THE MICHELIN FIELD GUIDE TO

MIN
ROCKS & FOSSILS

Note: Every effort has been made to ensure that the information contained in this Michelin Guide is as accurate and up-to-date as possible at the time of going to press. The authors, editors, consultants, and publishers of this book can not be held liable for any errors or omissions, nor for any consequences of using *The Michelin Field Guide to Minerals, Rocks, and Fossils*.

© I-Spy Limited 1997

ISBN 1 85671 186 2

Michelin Tyre Public Limited Company
Edward Hyde Building, 38 Clarendon Road, Watford, Herts WD1 1SX

MICHELIN and the Michelin Man are Registered Trademarks of Michelin

A CIP record for this title is available from the British Library.

Line Drawings by Will Giles and Sandra Pond.

Edited by Neil Curtis. Designed by Richard Garratt.

The Publisher gratefully acknowledges the contribution of Professor Richard Moody who provided the text and photographs in this Michelin Guide.

Colour reproduction by Anglia Colour.

Printed in Spain by Graficromo SA.

INTRODUCTION

This guide, divided into three sections, will resolve may of the questions you may have about the minerals, rocks, and fossils that occur naturally on our planet.

Minerals are composed of regularly arranged atoms, and they constitute the essential building blocks that form the Earth and its sister planets. Each mineral has its own chemical formula, and the orderly arrangement of its atoms results in its crystalline form. Beautiful examples of minerals can be seen in museums and private collections or frequently found in mining areas.

The most obvious evidence of the role of minerals as rock-builders is found in crystalline igneous rocks such as granites and microgranites. Here the presence of quartz, feldspars, and micas can be distinguished by colour, hardness, cleavage, and often by crystal form. These rocks are frequently very hard and resistant to weathering, and they are often used as kerb stones and facing slabs. Public buildings and large office blocks are wonderful sites to observe some of the most exotic rocks found on Earth.

Igneous, including volcanic, rocks are the products of the great processes that take place in the Earth's interior, and volcanoes are just outpourings of molten igneous rocks, generated at depth, through fractures at the surface.

In contrast, most sedimentary rocks are the products of erosion, with the processes associated with wind, rain, and ice, producing smaller and smaller grains and finer- and finer-grained sediments. Some sediments laid down in the sea are also products of erosion but others are formed chemically or by the accumulation and cementation of plant and animal remains.

The movement of the continents, and the collision of plates create huge changes in temperature and pressure, and igneous and sedimentary rocks can literally be baked and squeezed to form metamorphic rocks.

Fossils represent the history of life on Earth. The first simple plants, bacteria, and single-celled animals appeared 3.5 billion years ago. The first mineralized skeletons are found in rocks that are approximately 600 million years old – almost 4 billion years after the birth of our planet.

HOW TO USE THIS GUIDE

Geologists follow a code of practice which is intended to protect sites of scientific interest and limit damage to the environment. The emphasis on the search and discovery of minerals, rocks, and fossils has moved from collection to recognition and to the recording of sites. This does not mean that beautiful specimens cannot be obtained from areas across the globe, but care should be taken wherever you look for material. Great pleasure can be had from city walks, or a stroll around a mature cemetery where classic building stones have been used to enhance a building or to commemorate a life. Museums and jewellery offer access to rarer minerals and fossils, but many of those described in this book can be seen on coastal walks or visits to mines that are open to the general public. This book provides concise descriptions of some 250 of the best-known minerals, rocks, and fossils that occur naturally throughout Britain and the world.

The entries are arranged in order, with the minerals described in the groups that reflect their chemical composition; rocks are classified under the major headings of 'igneous', 'sedimentary', and 'metamorphic'; and fossils are divided essentially into plants, animals without backbones (invertebrates e g. clams or sea urchins), and vertebrates (such as reptiles or mammals). A short introduction to each grouping precedes the individual descriptions.

ESTABLISHING A COLLECTION

Bearing in mind the damage groups of individuals armed with hammers and chisels can do to a site, it is to be hoped that many collectors will gather specimens from mine waste tips or from rocks scattered along a coastal foreshore. High-quality specimens can also be bought from dealers but, again, we would caution you to ask how such specimens were obtained in the first place.

For those of us who enjoy fieldwork it is essential that we go prepared. Strong shoes, waterproof clothing, and a hard hat are important accessories throughout the year. These can be carried on-site in a good rucksack which should also contain plastic bags, kitchen roll, and marker pens for the registration and protection of your specimens. A hand lens is essential, and hammers and chisels may be used on approved sites. Care must be taken when hammering rocks; wear goggles! **Never** enter quarries or mine areas without permission and always wear your hard hat on-site.

The main rule of geology is to 'observe, measure, and record'. Collecting is fun, and you can establish an important collection of your own, by photographing, identifying, and cataloguing specimens in a logical and disciplined manner.

Your collection should be housed in a cabinet with shallow drawers, with each sample numbered and boxed individually. Never put too many specimens in one drawer and never put one on top of another. Index your material in a catalogue or on a computer. If you have access to the internet, you can now download images of minerals from specific web sites. Such images help in identification and can enhance the appearance of your collection. Be sure to clean your material regularly, but take special care about using water and other cleaning substances on softer, more clay-rich specimens. A dilute solution of washing-up liquid and a soft paint-brush are all that is needed to keep your collection in fine shape.

IN THIS I-SPY GUIDE

The minerals, rocks, and fossils illustrated are truly representative of the major groups that you will encounter on journeys and visits throughout Britain and Europe. Many of the rocks crop out in mountainous areas or along the foreshore, whereas others turn up in quarries and mines. Finding specimens is fun, and a unique mineral or fossil is often discovered by chance. The concise descriptions of each specimen should encourage you to read further, as many finds will differ slightly from those shown or you may even unearth something that has not been found before.

Individual minerals are named and given a chemical formula; each is also attributed to a crystal system. They are described in terms of colour, hardness, and fracture.

Rocks are described by texture and mineralogy, and colour, grain size, and field relationships are emphasized.

Fossils are associated with similar plants or animals, given a scientific name, and described in terms of size, form, and distribution in time and space.

MINERALS

Ancient civilizations appreciated that minerals were solid substances with a natural symmetry. Clear, glassy prisms of quartz were termed *krystallos* by people who believed that they had discovered 'permanent' ice crystals. The more sophisticated studies of latter-day scientists reveal that minerals are composed of atoms arranged in an orderly and fixed manner within an atomic lattice. The complete lattice is expressed in the beautiful crystals we find in the field or see in museums. It is also present in mineral fragments and exhibited in the crystalline form of many rocks.

Well-formed crystals have been allowed to grow over an extended period of time in a suitable medium. They are contained by crystal faces; these occur in sets (forms) which reflect a given symmetry. Regardless of shape or size, the crystal you find in the field conforms with the criteria set out above.

Minerals are divided into seven crystal systems. These are listed as cubic, tetragonal, trigonal, hexagonal, orthorhombic, monoclinic, and triclinic.

The **habit** of a crystal is controlled by the size and shape of its crystal faces. Elongate crystals are termed prismatic; flat ones tabular. **Colour** and **hardness** are also important in the identification of specific minerals. Talc can be scratched with a finger-nail, calcite with a knife, but diamonds are so hard that they are used to cut many other materials. Hardness is determined on a 1-to-10 scale. Colour is a diagnostic property although subtle colour differences may occur in specific minerals. **Streak** colours are determined when you drag a mineral across a piece of unglazed china. The trace left on the china (streak plate) is essentially the colour of the powdered mineral.

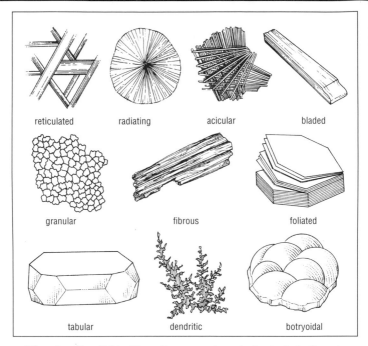

reticulated   radiating   acicular   bladed

granular   fibrous   foliated

tabular   dendritic   botryoidal

Minerals reflect light with a vitreous or glassy **lustre** typical of quartz or some micas. Gold has a metallic lustre.

Many minerals have inherent weaknesses in their atomic structures. In hand specimen, these weaknesses are expressed as **cleavage** planes. Calcite splits naturally into rhombs, for example, whereas mica occurs in thin sheets. Quartz, however, shatters on impact, and chert flakes into curved fragments exhibiting conchoidal **fractures**. **Twinned** crystals are frequently found in which two distinct growth areas divide at a common plane.

On the basis of their chemical composition, minerals are classified into two major groups: the silicates and the non-silicates. The silicates comprise a large group that includes quartz, garnet, mica, talc, feldspar, and topaz as representative minerals. Non-silicate minerals include the native elements such as gold and copper, oxides (corundum, magnetite), sulphides (pyrite), halides (rock salt), and oxygen salts such as phosphate and borax.

SILICATES	NON-SILICATES
single SiO4 groups (olivine, garnets)	**native elements** (copper, graphite)
ring silicates (tourmaline, beryl)	**oxides** (magnetite, corundum)
single chains pyroxenes (augite)	**sulphides** (pyrite, galena)
double chains or ribbons amphiboles (hornblende)	**halides** (rock salt, fluorite)
sheets (micas, chlorite, talc, clay minerals)	**oxygen salts** carbonates (calcite) sulphates (barytes) phosphates (apatite) borates (borax)
three-dimensional structures feldspars (orthoclase) feldspathoids (nepheline) silica group (quartz)	
miscellaneous silicates (aluminium silicates, zeolites, topaz, epidote)	

Native Elements

Native elements occur in a free state. Copper, gold, silver, and platinum are native metals; sulphur, graphite, and diamond are native non-metals. These elements originate in igneous (including volcanic) and metamorphic areas, but the more resistant forms, such as gold and diamonds, are often worked from stream deposits the world over.

Gold (Au)

Crystal system: Cubic.
Hardness: 2½–3.
Streak: Golden–yellow.
Cleavage: None.
Lustre: Metallic.
Habit: Dendritic, alluvial grains, cubic crystals.
Appearance and mineral facts: Gold is not common in the British Isles although mining is carried out in Wales, and stream deposits are known in Scotland. Gold is dense with a high specific gravity. It is ductile and malleable, and can be transported long distances downstream, with little effect. As a heavy mineral, it can be collected by panning after lighter minerals have been washed away. Gold is often found in association with quartz in mineralized veins. Fool's gold, or pyrite, is more brittle and much harder (6–6½).

Silver

(Ag)

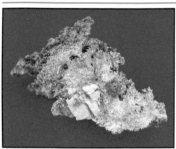

Crystal system: Cubic.
Hardness: 2½–3.
Streak: Silver–white.
Cleavage: None.
Lustre: Metallic.
Habit: Dendritic; massive, cubic crystals.

Appearance and mineral facts: Silver is usually associated with hydrothermal veins. The veins are formed when mineral-rich fluids cool or settle in fractures in the Earth's crust. Silver is often found in association with copper. Like gold, it is ductile and malleable and can be easily shaped. Silver, gold, and platinum are, therefore, the major elements used by jewellers. Note that cubic minerals have three axes at right-angles and of equal length.

Copper

(Cu)

Crystal system: Cubic.
Hardness: 2½–3.
Streak: Metallic pale copper-red.
Cleavage: None.
Lustre: Metallic.
Habit: Dendritic; cubic crystals.

Appearance and mineral facts: Copper is a native metal extensively used in the building of modern houses. It occurs naturally in areas of volcanic activity, where native copper fills gas cavities in basaltic

lavas. It also occurs as a cement in sedimentary rocks – copper-bearing fluids having migrated into the sediments from depth. Whereas silver has a black tarnish when weathered, copper goes a dull brown although a green patina is observed on a copper roof. Copper is malleable and ductile and has the same hardness as gold and silver.

Arsenic

(As)

Crystal system: Trigonal.
Hardness: 3½
Streak: Light grey.
Cleavage: Basal.
Lustre: Metallic–submetallic.
Habit: Massive.
Appearance and mineral facts: Arsenic occurs in association with silver and other ores in areas of hydrothermal activity. The crystals are found as

botryoidal and stalactitic masses, or they may be granular. Arsenic is light grey in its natural state. It tarnishes to dark grey, quickly losing its metallic lustre. Known throughout the ages as a poison, arsenic smells of garlic when fractured. Minerals belonging to the trigonal system have a single vertical axis and three other axes in the horizontal plane.

Antimony

(Sb)

Crystal system: Trigonal.
Hardness: 3–3½
Streak: Grey.
Cleavage: Basal.
Lustre: Metallic.
Habit: Kidney-shaped masses.
Appearance and mineral facts: Antimony, arsenic, and silver are frequently found together in hydrothermal veins. Crystals of all three are rare, and antimony normally occurs as kidney-shaped masses. It is

very light grey in colour and sometimes cleaves perfectly as distinct rhomb-like structures. More common minerals found with antimony in the field are pyrite and galena. Mining areas provide the usual hunting areas for these mineral associations. But permission and good practice in the field are essential to any visit.

Iron

(Fe)

Crystal system: Cubic.
Hardness: 4½.
Streak: White, steel grey.
Cleavage: Poor.
Lustre: Metallic.
Habit: Masses, grains, or meteorites.
Appearance and mineral facts:
Native iron is rare but can be found where coal seams are metamorphosed in contact with volcanic rocks. It is steel-grey to black in colour, and has a hackly fracture but no cleavage. Nickel-iron (NiFe) is a major constituent of meteorites. Iron is strongly magnetic. Iron deposits mined throughout the world are often associated with sedimentary rocks. Carbonates, oxides, and sulphates of iron may be formed as a result of the reaction between iron-rich waters and pre-existing rocks, or during the actual processes of sedimentation directly from iron-rich sea-water. Native iron is malleable.

Sulphur

(S)

Crystal system: Orthorhombic.
Hardness: 1½–2½.
Streak: White, pale yellow-white.
Cleavage: None.
Lustre: Resinous.
Habit: Tabular or bipyramidal crystals; massive, encrusting.
Appearance and mineral facts:
Sulphur often forms bright-yellow crystals, but brownish or translucent varieties also occur. The crystals are usually tabular or bipyramidal

although encrusting and stalactitic masses are associated with volcanic fumaroles or limestone areas. Sulphur is not hard and it will dissolve in carbon disulphide. It is a native non-metal. Crystals are normally associated with volcanic rocks. Sulphur occurs in salt-dome cap rocks in association with anhydrite, gypsum, and calcite. It is insoluble in water but does have a low melting point (113 °C). Orthorhombic crystals have three axes (mutually at right-angles) each of a different length.

Diamond

(C)

Crystal system: Cubic.
Hardness: 10.
Streak: None.
Cleavage: Perfect, octahedral.
Lustre: Adamantine, greasy when uncut.
Habit: Octahedral crystals; flattened crystals. Common twins.
Appearance and mineral facts: Diamond was named after the Greek word for 'invincible'. It is very hard and resistant to most natural forces. Diamonds occur in river and beach deposits, and in kimberlite pipes that originate deep down in the Earth's inner layers. It is often colourless, but white, green, brown, red, and black varieties are also known. The crystals have an adamantine lustre and are brilliant when cut. Gem-quality crystals contain no impurities or imperfections and are crystal clear. Diamonds are brittle and have a conchoidal fracture.

Graphite

(C)

Crystal system: Hexagonal.
Hardness: 1–2.
Streak: Black, shiny.
Cleavage: Basal, perfect.
Lustre: Metallic, dull.
Habit: Tabular, massive, flaky, commonly foliated, columnar.
Appearance and mineral facts: Although graphite and diamond have the same chemical composition, their structures and physical properties are very different. Graphite is soft with a dull metallic lustre; diamond is clear and very hard. Graphite is often a product of metamorphism but does occur naturally in pegmatite veins. It is greasy to touch, opaque, and black in colour. Graphite is used extensively in the manufacture of the 'lead' in pencils. In contrast, diamond is used to cut glass and other materials. Field acquaintance with graphite is usually through the handling of graphitic schists in areas such as Scotland and North Wales.

Sphalerite

(ZnS)

Crystal system: Cubic.
Hardness: 3½–4.
Streak: White–light yellow-brown.
Cleavage: Perfect.
Lustre: Adamantine, resinous.
Habit: Cubes, tetrahedrons, rhombdodecahedrons; fibrous, botryoidal, granular, massive.
Appearance and mineral facts: Commonly known as zinc blende or, by miners, as blende or Black Jack, sphalerite is the most common zinc mineral. It is found in association with galena in hydrothermal veins, and in ore bodies within limestone terrains. Sphalerite is yellow, brown, or black in colour and may be transparent to translucent. It is frequently found altered to limonite or smithsonite. Blende is often found on the spoil tips of mines scattered throughout the United Kingdom.

Chalcopyrite

(CuFeS$_2$)

Crystal system: Tetragonal.
Hardness: 3½–4.
Streak: Greenish-black.
Cleavage: Imperfect.
Lustre: Metallic.
Habit: Massive; tetrahedral, frequent twinning.

Appearance and mineral facts:
Chalcopyrite is found in porphyry copper deposits, and in igneous and metamorphic rocks. It is the most common copper mineral. It is readily distinguished, having a brassy yellow colour and brittle nature. When struck it has an uneven to conchoidal fracture. It is deeper yellow than pyrite, and often has an iridescent tarnish. Most finds are of massive crystal associations; individual perfectly formed tetrahedrons are rare. Tetragonal minerals are characterized by three axes, each at right-angles; one is vertical and of a different length to the other two.

Galena

(PbS)

Crystal system: Cubic.
Hardness: 2½.
Streak: Lead grey.
Cleavage: Cubic, perfect.
Lustre: Metallic.
Habit: Cubes, octahedrons; massive, granular.

Appearance and mineral facts: The name *galena* means 'lead ore'. It is the most important source of lead, and is found throughout the world in hydrothermal veins, and igneous and sedimentary rocks. Beautiful cubes and octahedrons are frequently found on spoil tips, especially where mineralization is associated with limestone or dolomitic rocks. Galena is lead grey in colour and opaque. Twinning of crystals is commonplace. In veins, galena is often found with quartz, calcite, baryte, and fluorite which are commonly referred to as gangue minerals. Galena can be altered, or oxidized, to produce cerussite and anglesite.

Stibnite

(Sb_2S_3)

Crystal system: Orthorhombic.
Hardness: 2.
Streak: Lead grey.
Cleavage: Perfect.
Lustre: Metallic.
Habit: Prismatic and acicular (needle-like) crystals.
Appearance and mineral facts: Stibnite is a compound of antimony found in areas of hot springs, hydrothermal veins, and in mineralized limestones. It is lead to steel grey in colour and opaque. Many crystals occur as radiating masses, and the colour becomes tarnished with a strong iridescence. The prismatic crystals have striae along their length. Stibnite is frequently found in association with galena and pyrite. Interestingly, it melts under a naked flame such as that from a cigarette lighter or match.

Marcasite

(FeS_2)

Crystal system: Orthorhombic.
Hardness: 6–6½
Streak: Grey–brownish-black.
Cleavage: Poor; prismatic.
Lustre: Metallic.
Habit: Tabular; radiating fibres, massive.
Appearance and mineral facts: Fresh crystals of marcasite have a pale, bronze-yellow colour. They are opaque and, when exposed to the elements, oxidize to ferrous sulphate, limonite, or pyrite. Marcasite can be found as concretions in chalk and as 'cock's-comb aggregates'. These are a result of crystal twinning, with the constituent crystals having a stacked triangular appearance. This shape is sometimes termed 'spearhead'. Marcasite is also found in hydrothermal veins in association with lead and zinc minerals. It is slightly paler than pyrite and chalcopyrite.

Pyrite

(FeS$_2$)

Crystal system: Cubic.
Hardness: 6–6½.
Streak: Green-black.
Cleavage: Poor.
Lustre: Metallic.
Habit: Cubes, massive, granular.
Appearance and mineral facts:
Pyrite or 'fool's gold' is one of
the best-known minerals. Cubes
are the more common crystal
form, with pyritohedrons and
octahedrons also regularly
recorded. The cubes are often

striated. Twinned, interpenetrative crystals are commonplace. Pyrite is a pale,
brassy yellow colour and opaque. It is soluble in nitric acid. Samples of pyrite
cubes occur in hydrothermal veins, and in metamorphic and sedimentary rocks.
Pyrite and chalcopyrite, and pyrite and gold are often associated.

Arsenopyrite

(FeAsS)

Crystal system: Monoclinic.
Hardness: 5½–6.
Streak: Grey-black.
Cleavage: Poor; brittle.
Lustre: Metallic.
Habit: Prismatic crystals;
massive.
Appearance and mineral facts:
Arsenopyrite, or mispickel, is the
most common arsenic mineral. It
is found in high-temperature
veins, associated with tin, and in
metamorphic areas. More rarely,
arsenopyrite occurs in limestones.

It is grey to silvery white in colour, and opaque. Twinning is commonplace,
with cross-shaped twins making fine specimens. Arsenopyrite is a high-
temperature mineral that forms early in the cooling of hydrothermal fluids. It is
found in veins, limestones, and schists.

Magnetite (Fe_3O_4)

Crystal system: Cubic.
Hardness: 5½–6½.
Streak: Black.
Cleavage: None.
Lustre: Metallic.
Habit: Octahedral crystals; massive, granular.
Appearance and mineral facts: Magnetite is strongly magnetic, and 'lodestone', which possesses a marked polarity, is used in the manufacture of compass needles. It is black, transparent, with an uneven to subconchoidal fracture. It is known from throughout the world, occurring in igneous rocks, high-temperature veins, and in areas of regional and contact metamorphism. Apart from octahedrons, rhombdodecahedral crystals are also known. Magnetite can occur in economically workable deposits.

Haematite (Hematite)

(Fe_2O_3)

Crystal system: Trigonal.
Hardness: 5–6.
Streak: Dark red.
Cleavage: None.
Lustre: Metallic, dull.
Habit: Massive, mammilate, and botryoidal masses; tabular crystals; fibrous.
Appearance and mineral facts: Haematite is known in several crystal forms, and commonly as mammillated or botryoidal masses, or

kidney ore. It is known from throughout the world, and is associated mainly with the mineralization of sedimentary rocks. It is also found in igneous and sedimentary rocks as an accessory mineral. Haematite has a brittle, uneven to subconchoidal fracture. It is non-magnetic and has a steel-grey to black colour. Haematite is used to manufacture red ochre and is a major source of iron ore.

Chromite

$(FeCr_2O_4)$

Crystal system: Cubic.
Hardness: 5½.
Streak: Dark brown.
Cleavage: None.
Lustre: Metallic–submetallic.
Habit: Octahedral crystals; massive, granular.
Appearance and mineral facts: Chromite is a member of the spinel group of minerals. It is rarely found in crystal form, and most discoveries are massive or granular in habit. It is

black to brownish black in colour, usually opaque with a metallic to submetallic lustre. Chromite is found in association with basic and ultrabasic rocks. Thick concentrations may occur, and these are often mined as the sole source of chromium. Chromite is heavy and resistant to transport and weathering, and it can be found as a heavy mineral in significant amounts in alluvial sands and gravels.

Corundum

(Al_2O_3)

Crystal system: Trigonal.
Hardness: 9.
Streak: None.
Cleavage: None.
Lustre: Adamantine–vitreous.
Habit: Flat, tabular, or spindle- or barrel-shaped crystals; massive, granular.
Appearance and mineral facts: Corundum is often found as emery, a massive granular variety which is black in colour and mixed with magnetite and spinel. The most common crystal shapes are tabular and pyramidal, the latter having steep sides and pointed ends. They are, in effect, spindle shaped whereas flat-ended crystal varieties are often barrel shaped. All three are found, abraded, in stream systems, the crystals developing a rough, pitted surface texture. Gemstone varieties, such as ruby and sapphire, occur in river gravels. Corundum is found in metamorphic areas and in pegmatites. It is valued as an abrasive and as a gemstone.

Ilmenite

$(FeTiO_3)$

Crystal system: Trigonal.
Hardness: 5–6.
Streak: Black.
Cleavage: None.
Lustre: Metallic–dull.
Habit: Tabular, rhombohedrons; massive, sand grains.
Appearance and mineral facts: Ilmenite is found in intermediate and basic igneous rocks, veins, and pegmatites. It is also commonly

found as a resistant, heavy mineral in beach sands. It is opaque and iron black in colour, with a brittle, conchoidal to subconchoidal fracture. Ilmenite is usually non-magnetic, and forms in the early stages of crystallization of igneous rocks. Commercially viable deposits are worked as a source of titanium. It is often associated with haematite and chalcopyrite.

Cassiterite

(SnO_2)

Crystal system: Tetragonal.
Hardness: 6–7.
Streak: White–pale grey.
Cleavage: Imperfect.
Lustre: Adamantine–submetallic.
Habit: Prismatic, bipyramids; massive.
Appearance and mineral facts: Cassiterite is a high-temperature mineral associated with hydrothermal veins. It is found in granitic regions, and occurs as commercially viable deposits in river gravels. It is the most important source of tin, and is especially well known from Malaysia. Cassiterite has a subconchoidal fracture, and is brown to black in colour; either opaque or almost transparent. Like other tetragonal minerals, cassiterite is characterized by three axes which are mutually perpendicular, with the vertical axis of a different length to the other two. Twinning is common in cassiterite. Several varieties of tinstone are known to miners, with fibrous, massive crystal deposits termed 'wood tin', and derived rounded pebbles, 'stream tin'.

Rutile

(TiO_2)

Crystal system: Tetragonal.
Hardness: 6–6½.
Streak: Pale brown.
Cleavage: Distinct–imperfect.
Lustre: Adamantine–submetallic.
Habit: Prismatic, pyramidal, needle-like; massive.
Appearance and mineral facts: Like ilmenite, rutile is an important source of titanium. It is red to red-brown in colour, and transparent to translucent in terms of opacity. Rarer black varieties are opaque. The fracture is brittle, uneven to subconchoidal, whereas cleavage is characteristically prismatic. Rutile is known throughout the world from igneous and metamorphic rocks. It also occurs in river deposits. Acicular, or needle-like, crystals are often present in quartz. Prismatic crystals have striated faces whereas bipyramidal crystals are often twinned.

Limonite

[FeO(OH)]

Crystal system: None.
Hardness: 5.
Streak: Yellow-brown.
Cleavage: None.
Lustre: Earthy, submetallic.
Habit: Botryoidal, massive, or as coatings or crusts.
Appearance and mineral facts: Limonite is the name given to a mixture of minerals, the main constituent of which is goethite. The name is also applied to weathered iron minerals the world over, and it is the most common colouring substance known in nature. It can occur as botryoidal or stalactitic masses but the ferruginous stains on rock surfaces are usually caused by the presence of limonite. It is a secondary mineral, an impure hydrated iron oxide, formed under surface conditions. Limonite is often associated with weathered ore deposits where the sulphides have been leached out.

Goethite

[FeO(OH)]

Crystal system: Orthorhombic.
Hardness: 5–5½.
Streak: Brownish yellow.
Cleavage: Perfect–brittle fracture.
Lustre: Adamantine–dull.
Habit: Massive, mammillated, botryoidal; rarely as prismatic or tabular crystals.
Appearance and mineral facts: Goethite is usually an earthy dark-brown colour. It is opaque and, unlike limonite, exhibits a cleavage and brittle fracture. Prismatic and tabular crystals are known but normally goethite is massive or stalactitic in form. Goethite is a product of oxidation, occurring mainly as a secondary mineral in weathered veins or in sedimentary rocks. 'Bog iron ore' is a form of goethite precipitated from fresh water in bogs or enclosed lagoons. Goethite becomes magnetic after exposure to a high heat source. It is known throughout the world.

Halite

(NaCl)

Crystal system: Cubic.
Hardness: 2½.
Streak: White.
Cleavage: Perfect.
Lustre: Vitreous.
Habit: Cubic crystals; massive, granular.
Appearance and mineral facts: Commonly known as rock salt, halite is a very common mineral. It is known throughout the world, and is formed by

the evaporation of sea-water in enclosed or restricted areas. Coastal sabkhas dotted along the shorelines of North Africa and the Middle East provide the ideal environments. Halite is frequently found as cubic crystals, some having hollow or indented faces, but massive, laminated deposits more than 250 metres thick are known. It is colourless and transparent, and very unstable. It can be recognized by taste, habit, and solubility. Halite is used in the manufacture of hydrochloric acid and sodium carbonate.

Fluorite

(CaF$_2$)

Crystal system: Cubic.
Hardness: 4.
Streak: White.
Cleavage: Perfect.
Lustre: Vitreous.
Habit: Cubic, octahedral and dodecahedral crystals; massive and granular.
Appearance and mineral facts: Also known as fluorspar, fluorite is known

from around the world. It is associated with hydrothermal veins and specific granites. Crystal masses are frequently found in lead-zinc deposits, with perfect, transparent cubes prized in the optical industries. The crystals are often coloured by impurities, and fluorite can adopt the colours of the rainbow. The highly coloured, banded Blue John of Derbyshire is much sought after by collectors. Fluorite has a brittle to subconchoidal fracture, and care should be taken when collecting in the field. Impure fluorite is used as a flux in the manufacture of steel.

Calcite

(CaCO₃)

Crystal system: Trigonal.
Hardness: 2½–3.
Streak: White.
Cleavage: Perfect parallel to rhomb shape.
Lustre: Vitreous.
Habit: Various crystal shapes; massive, fibrous, stalactitic, granular.
Appearance and mineral facts: Calcite is common throughout the world, and is associated with many rock types. It can be precipitated directly from sea-water, from the shells of invertebrate animals, or it may occur in mineralized veins. The most common crystal forms are nail-head, dog-tooth, and tabular. It is easily distinguished from quartz, another colourless, transparent mineral, by hardness, cleavage, and its solubility in dilute hydrochloric acid. Calcite can form under surface conditions as stalactites, travertine, or tufa. It is used as a flux in the smelting industry, and limestones or marble are used extensively in the construction industry.

Magnesite

(MgCO₃)

Crystal system: Trigonal.
Hardness: 3½–4½.
Streak: White.
Cleavage: Perfect.
Lustre: Vitreous–earthy.
Habit: Massive, fibrous; more rarely as crystals or grains.
Appearance and mineral facts: Magnesite occurs as a replacement mineral in limestones, and in areas where talc schists and serpentinite are common. It is usually massive or

fibrous in habit but rhombohedral and prismatic crystals are found occasionally. Normally white in colour, it can be stained shades of brown, yellow, or grey by impurities. Unlike calcite, it does not dissolve in dilute, cold hydrochloric acid. It has a higher specific gravity than either calcite or dolomite, and does not form twins. Magnesium-bearing fluids passing through limestones can result in the deposition of magnesite, and the dolomitization of the host rock.

Siderite

(FeCO₃)

Crystal system: Trigonal.
Hardness: 3½–4½.
Streak: White.
Cleavage: Perfect.
Lustre: Vitreous.
Habit: Rhombohedrons; massive, fibrous, botryoidal, granular. Twinned rhombohedrons.
Appearance and mineral facts: Siderite occurs as concretionary ironstones in claystones and as a

gangue mineral in ore deposits. It can also occur as layers, in limestones that have been affected by iron-rich fluids. Rhombohedral crystals are commonplace, but massive and fibrous varieties are more frequently encountered. The crystals have curved faces. Siderite is grey, grey-brown to yellowish brown in colour, and often translucent. Lamellar twins are common. It has a similar specific gravity to magnesite, and dissolves only slowly in cold dilute hydrochloric acid.

Rhodochrosite

(MnCO$_3$)

Crystal system: Trigonal.
Hardness: 3½–4.
Streak: White.
Cleavage: Perfect.
Lustre: Vitreous.
Habit: Massive, granular; rare rhombohedral crystals. Rarely twinned.
Appearance and mineral facts: Rhodochrosite is usually distinguished by its rose-pink colour, although light-grey and brown varieties are recorded. It can form exquisite rhombohedral crystals with curved faces, but mostly it is found in massive lumps. It occurs in mineralized veins associated with silver, copper, and lead, and in altered sedimentary rocks. It has an uneven fracture but cleaves easily. Rhodochrosite dissolves and effervesces in hot dilute hydrochloric acid. Transparent to translucent rhodochrosite blackens on exposure to the weather, a thin crust forming on the surface of the mineral.

Smithsonite

(ZnCO$_3$)

Crystal system: Trigonal.
Hardness: 4–4½.
Streak: White.
Cleavage: Perfect.
Lustre: Vitreous.
Habit: Botryoidal, kidney shaped, stalactitic; rare rhombohedrons.
Appearance and mineral facts: Smithsonite is associated with lead and zinc deposits, and may occur as a secondary or replacement mineral in sediments. It dissolves in warm

hydrochloric acid. Smithsonite can be shades of grey, brown, green, or yellow in colour with the yellow variety known as 'turkey-fat ore'; this last colour is associated with the presence of cadmium as an impurity. Smithsonite is a source of zinc, and its massive varieties are cut as ornamental stone. Green botryoidal masses and yellow-brown crystal masses are welcome additions to any mineral collection.

Dolomite

[CaMg(CO₃)₂]

Crystal system: Trigonal.
Hardness: 3½–4.
Streak: White.
Cleavage: Perfect.
Lustre: Vitreous–pearly.
Habit: Rhombs; massive, granular.

Appearance and mineral facts:
Unlike calcite, dolomite does not
dissolve readily in dilute hydrochloric
acid. Often white, dolomite can be
colourless, yellow, brown, or pink in colour. It has a subconchoidal fracture and a
very good rhombohedral cleavage. Dolomite can occur as perfect crystals in
hydrothermal veins or in limestones affected by magnesium-bearing fluids. It can
occur as a primary mineral in areas of continued evaporation such as sabkhas, or
replace limestones during early burial, shallow-burial, or deep-burial processes.
Dolomite occurs extensively worldwide throughout the geological record. It is used
to make high-temperature bricks and furnace linings, and cut for ornamental stone.

Aragonite

(CaCO₃)

Crystal system: Orthorhombic.
Hardness: 3½–4.
Streak: White.
Cleavage: Distinct.
Lustre: Vitreous.
Habit: Prisms, pyramids, tabular and
pseudohexagonal crystals; stalactitic,
encrusting.

Appearance and mineral facts:
Aragonite is a primary constituent of
many invertebrate skeletons, and is a precipitate directly from sea-water. It is
found around hot springs, and occurs in mineralized cavities in volcanic rocks
and in limestone areas that have also undergone mineralization. Aragonite is
metastable, however, and is replaced by calcite in early burial. It commonly
occurs as twins which are usually robust, with prisms capped by steep-sided
pyramids. The colour varies from colourless, white, and grey to yellowish in
transparent to translucent crystals. Aragonite dissolves in cold, dilute
hydrochloric acid.

Malachite

[Cu$_2$CO$_3$(OH)$_2$]

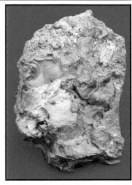

Crystal system: Monoclinic.
Hardness: 3½–4.
Streak: Pale green.
Cleavage: Perfect.
Lustre: Adamantine, silky–dull.
Habit: Botryoidal, stalactitic, encrusting, fibrous, granular.
Appearance and mineral facts: Malachite is an important copper ore, and often an outstanding semi-precious stone. Botryoidal, bright-green masses, cored with azurite, and cut and polished, are a must for most collectors. Crystals of malachite are rare but botryoidal and encrusting masses are commonly found as secondary deposits in oxidized zones associated with copper deposits. Malachite has an uneven to subconchoidal fracture. It is soluble in dilute hydrochloric acid. Crystals have an adamantine lustre whereas fibrous varieties are silky to dull.

Azurite

[Cu$_3$(CO$_3$)$_2$(OH)$_2$]

Crystal system: Monoclinic.
Hardness: 3½–4.
Streak: Light blue.
Cleavage: Perfect (prismatic), imperfect (pinacoidal).
Lustre: Vitreous.
Habit: Tabular, short prismatic crystals; radiating masses, massive.
Appearance and mineral facts: As its name suggests, azurite occurs as a deep-blue, transparent to translucent mineral. It is a secondary copper mineral which is known to form well-developed or sharp crystals. The crystals are tabular or prismatic. A conchoidal fracture and two cleavages are also characteristic. Azurite alters to malachite, and crystal pseudomorphs, where malachite has replaced azurite, are quite common. Unlike malachite, azurite is rather limited in terms of its world distribution, and is regarded as only a minor copper ore.

Ulexite

$(NaCaB_5O_9,8H_2O)$

Crystal system: Triclinic.
Hardness: 2½.
Lustre: Silky.
Streak: White.
Cleavage: Perfect, prismatic.
Habit: Parallel fibrous aggregates, rounded fibrous masses.
Appearance and mineral facts: Ulexite is white, fibrous, and silky in appearance. It is also transparent, and is sometimes termed the 'TV' mineral if impurities appear vaguely inside the mineral aggregate. Rounded fibrous masses are also termed 'cotton-balls'. The fine fibres are slightly soluble in hot water, and aggregates can be scored with a finger-nail. Ulexite is an evaporitic mineral frequently found in association with borax deposits. It is also found in geodes or solution cavities in sedimentary rocks, and as an evaporitic mineral in dried lakes in arid areas. In contrast, borax is often prismatic with a blue or grey coloration. Several borates, including ulexite and borax, can occur in association as linings in rock cavities.

Barytes (Baryte) $(BaSO_4)$

Crystal system: Orthorhombic.
Hardness: 3–3½.
Streak: White.
Cleavage: Perfect (basal), good (prismatic).
Lustre: Vitreous–pearly, earthy.
Habit: Tabular, prismatic; fibrous, lamellar, stalactitic, granular, aggregates.
Appearance and mineral facts: Baryte, barytes, or barite can form 'desert roses' or cock's-comb masses. Crystals can be colourless, transparent to opaque, but impurities associated with iron produce grey, yellowish, brown, red, pale-green, and pale-blue varieties. Baryte cleaves on two planes and has an uneven fracture. It occurs as a gangue mineral in hydrothermal veins, as a precipitate around hot springs, and as a cement in sedimentary rocks. Baryte has a high specific gravity and is distinguished by its weight.

Anhydrite

(CaSO$_4$)

Crystal system: Orthorhombic.
Hardness: 3–3½.
Streak: White.
Cleavage: Three good cleavages.
Lustre: Vitreous, pearly.
Habit: Massive, granular, fibrous.
Appearance and mineral facts:
Anhydrite is directly precipitated
from sea-water, and is commonly
found in association with halite and
gypsum. It is often associated with coastal sabkha environments where
temperatures in excess of 42 °C are the norm. It can occur as a primary or
secondary cement in sedimentary rocks, and is found commonly in
hydrothermal veins. Colours similar to those mentioned for baryte occur as a
result of impurities but anhydrite is normally transparent to translucent.
Anhydrite is used in the manufacture of sulphuric acid and plaster.

Gypsum

(CaSO$_4$.2H$_2$O)

Crystal system: Monoclinic.
Hardness: 2.
Streak: White.
Cleavage: Three (perfect to distinct)
give rise to lozenge-shaped 'chips'.
Lustre: Vitreous, pearly.
Habit: Tabular; fibrous, massive,
granular. 'Swallow-tail' and 'arrow-
head' twins.
Appearance and mineral facts:
Gypsum is often found as a rock-forming mineral in deposits that have been
produced as evaporites from saline waters. Thick, bedded sequences are known
from around the world. Individual crystals may be tabular, prismatic, or
diamond shaped. The faces are often curved. Twinning is very common, and the
crystals transparent to translucent. Yellow, grey, red, and brown colours occur
due to impurities. Gypsum can be scratched with a fingernail. It has three
cleavage planes, and is reduced to a powder on impact. Gypsum is commonly
formed with the hydration of anhydrite. Satin spar and 'desert roses' are two
outstanding examples of the habit assumed by this sulphate mineral.

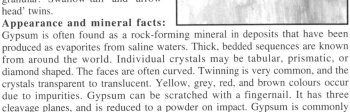

Wolframite

[(FeMn)WO$_4$]

Crystal system: Monoclinic.
Hardness: 5–5½.
Streak: Yellowy brown.
Cleavage: Perfect.
Lustre: Resinous, adamantine, submetallic.
Habit: Tabular, prismatic.
Appearance and mineral facts: Wolframite is found in mineralized veins and pegmatites in granitic areas, and less commonly in hydrothermal veins and alluvial sediments. It occurs as comparatively short, prismatic or tabular crystals which are yellow brown, reddish brown, dark greyish or brown-black in colour. The variable content of iron in the mineral can produce transparent to opaque varieties. An uneven fracture is characteristic. The more iron-rich varieties are weakly magnetic. Wolframite is a major source of tungsten, and is found in association with cassiterite, and galena and tourmaline.

Apatite

$[Ca_5(PO_4)_3(F,Cl,OH)]$

Crystal system: Hexagonal.
Hardness: 5.
Streak: White.
Cleavage: Imperfect.
Lustre: Vitreous.
Habit: Tabular or prismatic crystals; massive, granular, replacive.
Appearance and mineral facts: Apatite occurs in a range of igneous, metamorphic, and sedimentary rocks. It occurs as crystals in pegmatites, and is the main constituent of many phosphate deposits. Apatite is known in various guises throughout the world, and gem-quality crystals grace many collections. It is a major component of vertebrate skeletons, and can be concentrated in faecal pellets and nodules. Apatite can be scratched with a pen-knife, and has an uneven fracture. It dissolves in hydrochloric acid, and is used to produce 'superphosphate' on treatment with sulphuric acid.

Turquoise

$[CuAl_6(PO_4)_4(OH)_8.5H_2O]$

Crystal system: Triclinic.
Hardness: 5–6.
Streak: White, pale green.
Cleavage: Two distinct cleavages.
Lustre: Vitreous, waxy.
Habit: Rare, small, prismatic crystals; massive; cryptocrystalline.
Appearance and mineral facts: Turquoise is a semi-precious stone found as a secondary mineral in igneous and sedimentary rocks. It may occur as a pseudomorph of apatite and bone material. Crystals are rare. These are almost opaque, and sky blue to green in colour. Massive turquoise is characteristically blue in colour, and the quality of the sample may often be enhanced by cutting and polishing. The massive varieties have a waxy appearance whereas the small crystals are brighter and vitreous. Crystals cleave along two planes whereas massive turquoise has a conchoidal fracture.

Vanadinite

[Pb$_5$(VO$_4$)$_3$Cl]

Crystal system: Hexagonal.
Hardness: 3.
Streak: White–yellowish.
Cleavage: None.
Lustre: Sub-resinous–sub-adamantine.
Habit: Prisms, acicular crystals; encrusting.
Appearance and mineral facts: Vanadinite is an orange-red, brownish-red, orange-yellow coloured mineral, commonly found in limestones associated with lead mineralization. The quality of crystals varies but crusts of bright prismatic crystals are frequently found in mineralized cavities. It lacks a cleavage, and the fracture is uneven to conchoidal. Vanadinite is used in the steel industry and as a dye. Many of the samples available from mineral dealers originated in the Middle Atlas Mountains of Morocco. Large amounts of vanadinite are extracted from small addits in mineralized limestones.

Olivine

$[(MgFe)_2SiO_4]$

Crystal system: Orthorhombic.
Hardness: 6½–7.
Streak: White, grey.
Cleavage: Indistinct.
Lustre: Vitreous.
Habit: Granular, rock forming; rare small crystals.
Appearance and mineral facts: Typically, olivine is found in silica-poor basaltic and gabbroic rocks. It can be rock forming, and the rock dunite is 100 per cent olivine. Crystals of olivine are rare, and are usually olive green in colour and largely transparent, although yellowish, white, and brown to black varieties are known. The cleavage is indistinct and the fracture conchoidal. Olivine can be altered by hydrothermal fluids to form serpentine. Extra-terrestrial olivine is common in stony-iron meteorites, and in basalts found on the surface of the Moon.

Zircon

$(ZrSiO_4)$

Crystal system: Tetragonal.
Hardness: 7½.
Streak: White.
Cleavage: Indistinct.
Lustre: Adamantine, vitreous.
Habit: Prismatic with bipyramidal terminations. Common twinning.
Appearance and mineral facts: Zircon is hard with a high specific gravity. It has an indistinct cleavage and a conchoidal fracture. Crystals are usually brown to reddish brown,

but grey, green, violet, and even colourless varieties are known. They are transparent to translucent. Zircon is commonly found in granitic and syenite igneous rocks, with the largest crystals occurring in pegmatites. It is also found in river gravels as a resistant, heavy, detrital material. Zircon is valued as a gemstone, and is the major source of zirconium for industrial use.

Sphene

$(CaTiSiO_5)$

Crystal system: Monoclinic.
Hardness: 5–5½.
Streak: White.
Cleavage: Good, prismatic.
Lustre: Adamantine, resinous.
Habit: Flattened and wedge-shaped crystals; massive, lamellate.
Appearance and mineral facts: Perfect crystals of sphene are cut to produce brilliant gemstones. They can be brown, yellow, green, or grey in colour, transparent to opaque. Sphene is found as an accessory mineral in the more silica-rich

igneous rocks, in metamorphic schists, and in metamorphosed limestones. Sphene has a conchoidal fracture, and the resinous to adamantine lustre is one of its distinctive features. Like staurolite, sphene is often found in the form of cross-shaped twins. It occurs throughout the world.

Andalusite

(Al_2SiO_2)

Crystal system: Orthorhombic.
Hardness: 6½–7½.
Streak: White.
Cleavage: Good.
Lustre: Vitreous.
Habit: Prismatic, cruciform; massive.
Appearance and mineral facts:
Andalusite is found in rocks that have undergone regional and thermal metamorphism. It is particularly abundant, in crystal form, in cordierite hornfels which can be found in direct contact with igneous intrusions. The crystals are often rectangular prisms, but cross-shaped twins may occur if the variety chiastolite (*inset*) is present. White mica flakes are often produced by the alteration of andalusite. Andalusite has a distinct cleavage, subconchoidal fracture, and occurs in a variety of colours, including pink, red, brown, green, and yellow.

Kyanite

(AlSiO$_5$)

Crystal system: Triclinic.
Hardness: 5½–7.
Streak: White.
Cleavage: Two, good–perfect.
Lustre: Vitreous.
Habit: Flat, bladed, radiating.
Appearance and mineral facts: The more elongate crystals of kyanite can be bent because of an inherent flexibility. Kyanite crystals

are usually blue or white in colour, but grey and green varieties are known. They are transparent to translucent. The mineral is found in coarse-grained pegmatites, quartz veins, and commonly in rocks affected by regional metamorphism. Kyanite schists are noted for the presence of sky-blue, bladed crystals and/or porphyroblasts. The bladed crystals often lie parallel to the foliation of the rock.

Sillimanite

(Al$_2$SiO$_5$)

Crystal system: Orthorhombic.
Hardness: 6½–7½.
Streak: White.
Cleavage: Perfect, pinacoidal.
Lustre: Vitreous, silky.
Habit: Prismatic crystals; fibrous masses.
Appearance and mineral facts: Sillimanite is a fibrous silicate usually found in rocks that have undergone high-

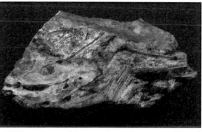

grade, regional metamorphism. Sillimanite schists and gneisses are found throughout the world, and have medium- to coarse-grained textures. Sillimanite crystals are usually very fine and needle-like in appearance. They can be colourless, but white, pale-yellow, and brownish varieties also occur. The variety fibrolite can be found in gemstone quality. Crystals of sillimanite are transparent to translucent, and there are distinct striations along their length.

Staurolite

$[(FeMg)_2(AlFe)_9Si_4O_{22}(O,OH)_2]$

Crystal system: Monoclinic, pseudo-orthorhombic.
Hardness: 7–7½.
Streak: Grey.
Cleavage: Good.
Lustre: Vitreous, resinous.
Habit: Prismatic, cruciform twins; massive.
Appearance and mineral facts: The cross-shaped crystals are a distinctive feature of a mineral that gets its name from the Greek word for 'cross'. The crystals often have a rough surface texture, and are reddish brown to brown-black in colour. They are translucent to opaque, and give a grey streak. The cleavage is distinct, and there is an uneven to subconchoidal fracture. This mineral is found in staurolite schists which are the products of high-grade metamorphism. It occurs as crystals and as porphyroblasts.

Topaz

[AlSiO$_4$(OH,F)$_2$]

Crystal system: Orthorhombic.
Hardness: 8.
Streak: None.
Cleavage: Perfect.
Lustre: Vitreous.
Habit: Prismatic; massive, granular.
Appearance and mineral facts: Topaz is hard with a distinct cleavage, and a subconchoidal to uneven fracture. Pink-coloured crystals are rare, but pale-yellow, pale-blue, and green-coloured varieties are used as gemstones. Topaz is found in pegmatites, quartz veins, and in rhyolitic rocks. It is resistant to weathering and erosion, and is found in river sediments. It is associated with tourmaline, fluorite, apatite, and beryl in pegmatitic veins. Strangely, some topaz crystals lose their colour when continuously exposed to strong sunlight.

Garnet – Pyrope

$(Mg_3Al_2Si_3O_{12})$

Crystal system: Cubic.
Hardness: 6½–7½.
Streak: White.
Cleavage: None.
Lustre: Vitreous, resinous.
Habit: Common well-formed crystals; massive, granular.

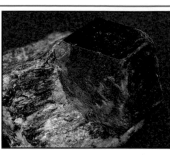

Appearance and mineral facts: Pyrope has been chosen as an example of the garnet group of minerals. Other common varieties are almandine, spessartine, hesonite, and grossular. Garnet crystals are commonly found in metamorphic rocks such as schists and gneisses, and less frequently in igneous rocks such as peridotite and granite. Pyrope is found in basic to ultrabasic rocks. It is deep red, brown, to blackish brown in colour, and transparent to translucent. It has no cleavage but the fracture is subconchoidal. Garnets are used in abrasives, and complete, unflawed crystals can be cut as gemstones.

Epidote

$[Ca_2(AlFe)_3Si_3O_{12}(OH)]$

Crystal system: Monoclinic.
Hardness: 6–7.
Streak: White, grey-white.
Cleavage: Perfect.
Lustre: Vitreous.
Habit: Prismatic crystals; massive, fibrous, granular.

Appearance and mineral facts: Epidote, and its sister mineral clinozoisite, belong to the monoclinic system. Crystals are common, and epidote is yellow-green to black in colour, while clinozoisite is pale green to greenish grey. Each has an uneven fracture and can be transparent to almost opaque. Many crystals have deep striae along their length. Epidote and clinozoisite are found in low-grade and contact metamorphic rocks. Metamorphosed basalts and limestones are frequently rich in epidote minerals. They also occur in veins in igneous rocks.

Spodumene

$(LiAlSi_2O_6)$

Crystal system: Monoclinic.
Hardness: 6½–7.
Lustre: Vitreous.
Streak: White.
Cleavage: Perfect.
Habit: Striated prismatic crystals; massive, columnar.
Appearance and mineral facts:
Spodumene crystals up to 15 metres, and approximately 85 tonnes in weight are known. Most crystals are of hand-specimen size, commonly

twinned with a perfect cleavage and splintery fracture. Various species of spodumene are found. The most common is greyish white in colour. Kunzite is lilac in colour and transparent to translucent. Like tourmaline and beryl, spodumene and its sister minerals are found in granite pegmatites. Kunzite is used as a gemstone and is mined as a lithium ore.

Wollastonite

$(CaSiO_2)$

Crystal system: Triclinic.
Hardness: 4½–5.
Streak: White.
Cleavage: Three.
Lustre: Vitreous, silky.
Habit: Fibrous masses, short prismatic and tabular crystals, granular.
Appearance and mineral facts:
Wollastonite has a silicon-oxygen tetrahedron-based structure which is

distinct from the linked chains found in pyroxenes. It commonly occurs as fibrous or needle-like masses, and is associated in the field with contact and high-grade regional metamorphism. Clusters of fibres are associated with metamorphosed limestones, and small, well-formed crystals are present in igneous rocks. Cleavage occurs on three planes, one of which is a perfect cleavage. It has an uneven fracture. Crystals have a vitreous lustre, and, in terms of opacity, can be subtransparent to translucent.

Beryl

$(Be_3Al_2Si_6O_{18})$

Crystal system: Hexagonal.
Hardness: 7½–8.
Streak: White.
Cleavage: Poor.
Lustre: Vitreous.
Habit: Prismatic crystals; massive.
Appearance and mineral facts:
Beryl is frequently formed in
pegmatites, hydrothermal veins,
schists, and gneisses. Crystal sizes
vary dramatically, and specimens of 5.4 metres in length have been found in
pegmatites. Beryl forms in a range of colours, but gem-quality beryl is usually
light to dark green, yellow, or bluish green. These stones are transparent, but
poorer-quality beryl can be translucent. Beryl has a poor basal cleavage, and an
uneven to conchoidal fracture. Emerald is a dark-green variety of beryl. Striae
may occur along the length of elongate crystals.

Cordierite

$[(MgFe)_2Al_4Si_5O_{18}]$

Crystal system: Orthorhombic.
Hardness: 7–7½.
Streak: White.
Cleavage: Poor.
Lustre: Vitreous.
Habit: Massive, granular; rare prismatic crystals.
Appearance and mineral facts: Cordierite is essentially associated with metamorphic rocks in areas that have undergone high-grade, contact or regional metamorphism. Andalusite cordierite hornfelses are known throughout the world and, in contrast to andalusite, cordierite is usually represented by rounded grains rather than by well-formed crystals. Prismatic and pseudohexagonal crystals are known, the latter forming as a result of repeated twinning. Clear cordierite crystals are used as gemstones. There is a poor cleavage, and the fracture is uneven to subconchoidal. Dark-blue to greenish-blue varieties occur, and they are transparent to translucent.

Tourmaline

$[Na(Mg)_3Al_6(Bo)_3Si_6O_{18}]$
(variable composition)

Crystal system: Trigonal.
Hardness: 7–7½.
Streak: None.
Cleavage: Very poor.
Lustre: Vitreous.
Habit: Prismatic, parallel–radiating
crystal groups.

Appearance and mineral facts:
Tourmaline is locally abundant in
pegmatites and granites, and less
common in schists, gneisses, and
metamorphosed limestones. It is

often found as elongate, striated crystals of semi-precious gemstone quality.
Colours range from black to pink with many crystals zoned along their length.
Tourmaline has a very poor cleavage, and an uneven to conchoidal fracture. The
chemical composition of this mineral is extremely variable. Crystals of
tourmaline are used in the production of pressure gauges. Tourmaline crystals
5–8 centimetres long are commonplace.

Idocrase

$[Ca_{10}(Mg)_2Al_4Si_9O_34(OH,F)]$
(variable composition)

Crystal system: Tetragonal.
Hardness: 6–7.
Streak: White.
Cleavage: Poor.
Lustre: Vitreous to resinous.
Habit: Short, prismatic, pyramidal
crystals; massive, granular.

Appearance and mineral facts:
Idocrase is found in blocks of limestone
thrown out during the eruptions of Mount
Vesuvius in Italy. Consequently, it is also
given the name vesuvianite. It has a very
variable composition in which specific
elements readily replace one another.

Tetragonal crystals occur in green, dark-green, brown, yellowish, and blue
varieties. They are transparent to translucent with an uneven to conchoidal
fracture. Clusters of crystals may occur in metamorphosed limestones.

Diopside

$[Ca(MgFe)Si_{12}O_6]$

Crystal system: Monoclinic.
Hardness: 5½–6½.
Streak: White–grey.
Cleavage: Good.
Lustre: Vitreous.
Habit: Prismatic; massive, granular.
Appearance and mineral facts: Diopside is a member of the pyroxene group of minerals in which the basic structure consists of silicon-oxygen tetrahedrons arranged in chains. This form of packing gives rise to two cleavages. Diopside is a pyroxene with the element calcium in the structure, as has augite (below). Diopside is pale green to grey in colour, and translucent to opaque. It forms as stout prisms, and twinning is common. Diopside occurs in skarns, metamorphosed limestones, and, more rarely, in basalts.

Augite

$[(Ca,Mg,Fe,Ti,Al)(Al,Si)_2O_6]$

Crystal system: Monoclinic.
Hardness: 5½–6½.
Streak: White–grey.
Cleavage: Good.
Lustre: Vitreous.
Habit: Short, prismatic crystals.
Appearance and mineral facts: Augite is a dark-green to black pyroxene containing calcium. It has good cleavages and an uneven fracture. Good crystals are relatively common, and small, square, to eight-sided specimens are found in basic to ultrabasic rocks. Twinned crystals appear to be longer with a V-shaped notch at the end. Augite is the most common ferromagnesium mineral in igneous rocks, and is found throughout the world. Basalts, andesites, and gabbroic rocks yield good examples of this pyroxene.

Actinolite (Tremolite)

$[Ca_2(Mg,Fe)_5Si_8O_{22}(OH)_2]$

Crystal system: Monoclinic.
Hardness: 5.6.
Streak: White.
Cleavage: Good.
Lustre: Vitreous.
Habit: Long prismatic crystals; aggregates, massive, fibrous.
Appearance and mineral facts: Actinolite and tremolite form a series of amphiboles with varying iron content. Actinolite is found in low-grade metamorphic rocks that were originally basalts, andesites, or claystones. Actinolite is usually green, and transparent to translucent. It has good prismatic cleavage and no fracture. Dark-green ornaments are often produced from nephrite, a variety of actinolite. Tremolite is the more common of the amphiboles, and both are common in magnesium-rich rocks.

Hornblende

$[(Ca,Na)_{2-3}(Mg,Fe)_5(Si,Al)_8O_{22}(OH)_2]$
(variable composition)

Crystal system: Monoclinic.
Hardness: 5–6.
Streak: White, grey.
Cleavage: Good, prismatic.
Lustre: Vitreous.
Habit: Prismatic, six-sided crystals; massive, granular.
Appearance and mineral facts: Hornblende occurs in igneous and metamorphic rocks. It has a variable chemical composition, and varies in colour from light green to almost

black. Darker varieties tend to occur in more basic rocks. It exhibits a good prismatic cleavage but has an uneven fracture. Short, prismatic crystals are commonplace; they are translucent to almost opaque. Hornblende is found in granodiorites, diorites, syenites, gabbros, and in regionally metemorphosed areas where the rocks are amphibolites and hornblende schists.

Glaucophane

$[Na_2(Mg,Fe,Al)_5Si_8O_{22}(OH)_2]$
(variable composition)

Crystal system: Monoclinic.
Hardness: 5–6.
Streak: White–blue-grey.
Cleavage: Good, prismatic.
Lustre: Vitreous, silky.
Habit: Fibrous aggregates.
Appearance and mineral facts: Glaucophane and riebeckite form a series within the amphibole group of minerals, with magnesium and aluminum replacing iron. Glaucophane is characteristic of

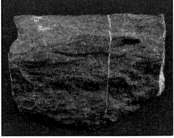

schists formed under low-temperature regional metamorphism. Good crystals are rare. Glaucophane crystals are translucent to subtranslucent; grey, grey-blue, and lavender-blue in colour. They exhibit a good cleavage and uneven fracture. Blue asbestos is a variety of riebeckite, and is known as crocidolite. Silicified crocidolite becomes golden brown; it is known as tiger-eye.

Muscovite

$[KAl_2(AlSi_3O_{10})(OH)_2]$

Crystal system: Monoclinic.
Hardness: 2½–4.
Streak: White.
Cleavage: Perfect.
Lustre: Vitreous, pearly.
Habit: Tabular crystals; lamellar masses and flakes.
Appearance and mineral facts: Muscovite, like other micas, is characterized by a distinct cleavage which gives rise to tiny flakes. Mica is colourless or pale green, brownish, and transparent to translucent. The flakes are flexible. Muscovite occurs in granites and pegmatites, and in schists and gneisses formed under low-grade to medium-grade metamorphism. Large clusters, or 'books', of muscovite are often found in pegmatite veins. Secondary muscovite, or sericite, is formed when feldspars decompose. Detrital muscovite is found in some fine-grained sediments.

Biotite

$[K(MgFe)_3AlSi_3O_{10}(OH)_2]$

Crystal system: Monoclinic.
Hardness: 2–3.
Streak: White, grey.
Cleavage: Perfect.
Lustre: Vitreous, pearly.
Habit: Tabular or short, pseudohexagonal crystals; lamellar aggregates, flakes.
Appearance and mineral facts: Biotite is a greenish-black, dark-brown, or black mica that occurs in pegmatites, granites, syenites, and diorites. It is also common in schists and gneisses. 'Books' of biotite cleave into thin, flexible plates. The name biotite is often used as a 'sack' term for all forms of dark mica. Phlogopite is a closely associated variety which occurs in metamorphosed limestones and magnesium-rich rocks. It is pale green to brown in colour, with a coppery hue.

Glauconite

$[K(Fe,Mg,Al)_2(Si_4O_{10})(OH)_2]$
(variable composition)

Crystal system: Monoclinic.
Hardness: 2.
Streak: Green.
Cleavage: Perfect.
Lustre: Dull, earthy.
Habit: Grains, aggregate.
Appearance and mineral facts: Glauconite is found in sedimentary rocks. It usually occurs as rounded grains or aggregates, but rock-forming accumulations are known.

Phosphate is commonly associated with glauconite in marine sediments. Grains may be green to black in colour, and are usually opaque to translucent. Celadonite, a closely related form, occurs in vesicular basalts. Glauconite is particularly abundant in inner and mid-platform sandstones and limestones, but may be carried downslope into deeper-water environments.

Lepidolite

$[K(Li,Al)_3(SiAl)_4O_{10}(OH)_2]$

Crystal system: Monoclinic.
Hardness: 2½–3.
Streak: None.
Cleavage: Perfect.
Lustre: Vitreous, pearly.
Habit: Flakes; tabular, pseudohexagonal crystals.
Appearance and mineral facts: Like glauconite, lepidolite has a variable composition, with variations in the percentages of

potassium, sodium, lithium, and other elements. Lepidolite may be colourless, pale lilac, pink, grey, or pale yellow, and is transparent to translucent. It occurs as crystals or as small flakes associated with a perfect basal cleavage. Lepidolite is found in granite pegmatites. It is a source of lithium, and is used in the manufacture of glass and ceramics.

Chlorite

$[(Mg,Fe,Al)_6(Al,Si)_4O_{10}(OH)_8]$
(variable composition)

Crystal system: Monoclinic.
Hardness: 2–3.
Streak: White, pale green.
Cleavage: Perfect.
Lustre: Vitreous, earthy.
Habit: Tabular, pseudohexagonal, prismatic crystals; aggregates, massive.
Appearance and mineral facts: Chlorite is widely known from igneous, metamorphic, and sedimentary rocks. It can result from the alteration of pyroxenes, amphiboles, and micas in igneous rocks, or may precipitate in the amygdales of basaltic lavas. It is green in colour, although the presence of magnesium and chromium can result in orange-brown or violet varieties. Cleavage results in small flakes but, in contrast to muscovite and biotite, these are flexible but not elastic. Chlorite schists have a well-developed schistosity. They are formed from the metamorphism of fine-grained rocks or pelites.

Serpentine

$[Mg_3Si_2O_5(OH)_4]$

Crystal system: Monoclinic.
Hardness: 2½–4.
Streak: White.
Cleavage: Perfect.
Lustre: Waxy, greasy, silky.
Habit: Massive, fibrous, lamellate, platy.
Appearance and mineral facts: Serpentine is actually the name given to a group of minerals which includes the fibrous chrysotile, the lamellate or

platy antigorite, lizardite, and garnierite. Chrysotile is an asbestiform mineral used in the manufacture of asbestos cements. It has a silky lustre, no cleavage, and no fracture. Massive serpentinites are formed by the alteration of olivine-rich igneous rocks such as basalts. The massive varieties have a waxy or greasy lustre. They occur in shades of green and are extensively used as decorative or monumental stone. Outcrops of serpentinite are found on the Lizard peninsula in Cornwall.

Talc

$[Mg_3Si_4O_{10}(OH)_2]$

Crystal system: Monoclinic.
Hardness: 1.
Streak: White, pale green.
Cleavage: Perfect.
Lustre: Dull, pearly.
Habit: Granular, massive; rare crystals.
Appearance and mineral facts: Commonly known as soapstone, talc is extremely soft with a dull or pearly lustre. It occurs as an alteration product after olivine, pyroxene, or amphibole in low-grade metamorphic rocks and in metamorphosed dolomites. Massive soapstone is used in the cosmetics, electrical, and paint industries. Crystals are rare. Talc is normally white to pale green in colour, but grey and red-brown varieties have also been recorded. It is translucent, and the pearly lustre is found on the perfect basal cleavage surface.

Quartz

(SiO$_2$)

Crystal system: Trigonal.
Hardness: 7.
Streak: White.
Cleavage: None.
Lustre: Vitreous.
Habit: Six-sided prisms; massive. Common twinning.
Appearance and mineral facts: Quartz is one of the most abundant and widespread of all minerals. It occurs in igneous, metamorphic, and sedimentary rocks, and in various types of veins and fractures. Crystals are commonplace and, although white or colourless varieties are the most common, amethyst, citrine, rose and smoky quartz are well known as semi-precious stones. Quartz has no cleavage but is noted for its conchoidal fracture. Twinning is common. Crystals are transparent to translucent. Excellent bipyramidal crystals commonly occur in evaporites or quartz-rich sandstones.

Chalcedony

(SiO$_2$)

Crystal system:
Cryptocrystalline.
Hardness: 6½.
Streak: White.
Cleavage: None.
Lustre: Vitreous, waxy.
Habit: Massive, mammillate, botryoidal, stalactitic.
Appearance and mineral facts: Chalcedony is a

uniformly coloured form of quartz made up of microscopic crystals. It is frequently banded, and is commonly found as mammillate or botryoidal masses. It varies in colour, with white, red, brown, green, and yellow varieties commonplace. These have different names: jasper is red and opaque; flint is dark brown and translucent. Chalcedony is deposited from silica-rich fluids, and occurs frequently as a fill or lining of cavities or fissures. In hot springs and volcanic areas, it can impregnate woody tissues or replace the mineralized shells and bones of invertebrates and vertebrates.

Agate

(SiO$_2$)

Crystal system:
Cryptocrystalline.
Hardness: 6½–7.
Streak: White.
Cleavage: None.
Lustre: Vitreous–waxy.
Habit: Cavity linings.
Appearance and mineral facts: Agate is a banded or layered variety of chalcedonic silica. It is commonly found as cavity linings in volcanic

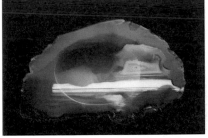

rocks. These geodes can vary in size, shape, and colour, with the banded agate passing inwards into well-formed quartz crystals. Hollow and filled geodes are collected as semi-precious stones and cut as ornaments. Moss agate has an irregular, moss-like patterning caused by the presence of mineral impurities. Agate purchased in mineral shops may have been stained.

Opal

(SiO₂.nH₂O)

Crystal system: Amorphous, submicrocrystalline.
Hardness: 5½–6½.
Streak: White.
Cleavage: None.
Lustre: Vitreous, resinous.
Habit: Massive, botryoidal, stalactitic, rounded.
Appearance and mineral facts: Opal may be colourless, white, grey, red, brown, green, blue, or almost black in colour. It is transparent to subtranslucent, with a conchoidal fracture. It is formed from low-temperature, silica-rich fluids, and is a common vein-filling or replacement mineral around hot springs and geysers. Opal is valued as a gemstone. The opaline siliceous skeletons of diatoms can form thick sedimentary sequences in freshwater lakes associated with volcanic areas. The sediments are quarried for use as industrial abrasives.

Orthoclase

(KAlSi$_3$O$_8$)

Crystal system: Monoclinic.
Hardness: 6–6½.
Streak: White.
Cleavage: Two,
perfect–good.
Lustre: Vitreous, pearly.
Habit: Prismatic, flattened,
or elongate.
**Appearance and mineral
facts:** Orthoclase is a
potassic feldspar which is
normally white or pale pink

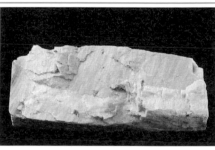

in colour. It is transparent to subtranslucent, with two perfect cleavages and an
uneven to conchoidal fracture. Several types of twin are known, with carlsbad,
baveno, and mannebach varieties as collectors' items. Orthoclase is present in
most igneous and metamorphic rocks. Its high-temperature equivalent, sanidine,
is often colourless or grey, tabular in habit, and is associated with volcanic and
thermally metamorphosed rocks.

Labradorite

Crystal system: Triclinic.
Hardness: 6–6½.
Streak: White.
Cleavage: Two, good.
Lustre: Vitreous, pearly.
Habit: Prismatic, tabular crystals;
massive, granular.
Appearance and mineral facts:
Labradorite is a plagioclase feldspar
which also exhibits several types of
twinning. It has two good cleavages
and an uneven fracture. Labradorite
exhibits an excellent range of blue
and green colours which can appear

iridescent in the right light. Plagioclase feldspars also exhibit repeated twinning
with twin lamellae visible on one of the two cleavage surfaces. Labradorite is
found in layered gabbroic rocks.

Nepheline

$(NaAlSiO_4)$

Crystal system: Hexagonal.
Hardness: $5\frac{1}{2}$–6.
Streak: White.
Cleavage: Two, indistinct.
Lustre: Vitreous, greasy.
Habit: Six-sided prisms; granular.
Appearance and mineral facts: Nepheline crystals are usually white, grey, or colourless but greenish and brownish-red varieties occur more rarely. They are transparent to translucent. It is found in plutonic and volcanic rocks which are usually alkaline and poor in silica. Nepheline syenites and phonolite lavas are typical examples of rock types.

Lazurite

$[(Na,Ca)_8(AlSi)_{12}O_{24}4(S,SO_4)]$

Crystal system: Cubic.
Hardness: 5½–6.
Streak: Bright blue.
Cleavage: None.
Lustre: Vitreous.
Habit: Massive; rare crystals.
Appearance and mineral facts: Lazurite crystals are usually azure blue and transluscent. They are rare and usually occur as cubes. The mineral is found in contact metamorphic regions where limestones are in contact with igneous rocks. Lapis lazuli contains an abundance of lazurite. It is often of gemstone quality and is extensively used in the manufacture of jewellery.

Stilbite

$[NaCa_2(Al_5Si_{13})O_{36}.14H_2O]$

Crystal system: Monoclinic.
Hardness: 3½–4.
Streak: White.
Cleavage: Perfect.
Lustre: Vitreous, pearly.
Habit: Aggregates of twinned crystals.
Appearance and mineral facts: Zeolites comprise a diverse group of alumino-silicate minerals which are often fibrous in habit. Tabular, rhombohedral, and other crystal forms occur, but the main common feature is that zeolites have free water held in pores within their overall structure. Stilbite occurs as aggregates of twinned crystals. These are often white with, less frequently, pink, yellowish, or red. The mineral is commonly found in voids or cavities in basaltic rocks.

Natrolite

$(Na_2Al_2Si_{13}O_{10} \cdot 2H_2O)$

Crystal system: Orthorhombic.
Hardness: 5–5½.
Streak: White.
Cleavage: Perfect, prismatic.
Lustre: Vitreous.
Habit: Prisms, needles, radiating masses. Rare twinning.
Appearance and mineral facts: Natrolite can easily be confused with other fibrous zeolites. Like stilbite, it occurs in cavities in basaltic lavas, but it is harder. Mesolite and scolecite are similar in composition to natrolite but occur only as fibrous aggregates – never as distinct prismatic crystals. Thomsonite is also a fibrous zeolite, but it has a different chemical composition, and it is coarsely crystalline. Natrolite has a perfect prismatic cleavage, and is transparent to translucent.

ROCKS

The history of the solar system is, in effect, written in the rocks that form the Earth and the other planets. On Earth, the first rocks were formed more than 4.5 billion years ago, soon after the 'Big Bang'. Naturally occurring elements gave rise to mineral compounds, and aggregates of minerals formed the first rocks. Since then, the primary source of rock material has been molten magma which migrates upwards from the Earth's mantle. Volcanoes are a surface expression of the great processes and forces that continue to exist deep below our feet. Lava flows and granitic intrusions reflect the compositions of the original magma, primary crystallization from the original melt or fluid resulting in an association of minerals with a particular texture. The term, 'igneous', is applied to rocks formed essentially by primary crystallization. Magmas may originate as deep within the Earth as 200 kilometres (125 miles) below the surface at temperatures in excess of 1000 °C.

The weathering of the first igneous rocks began almost immediately they were formed, and there is little doubt that some were consumed or modified during the formation of the early crust. 'Sedimentary' rocks are the product of weathering, erosion, and deposition, or chemical precipitation. In contrast to the origins of igneous rocks, sediments, such as sandstones and limestones, are formed under near-atmospheric pressures and in temperatures that rarely exceed 100 °C. The solid recrystallization of igneous and sedimentary rocks through deep burial or through a rise in temperature is termed 'metamorphism'. As

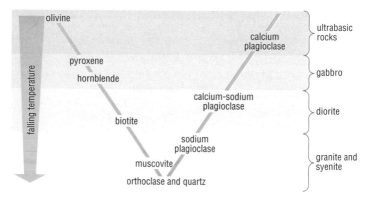

Order of crystallization of minerals from magmas.

temperatures and pressures change, the original minerals will change and stabilize to reflect their new environment. Textural changes are inevitable in rocks that are subjected to temperatures of 100–900 °C, and flow and compressional features are characteristic of many metamorphic rocks.

Rocks are studied by petrologists. Such scientists are interested in the mineralogy and the textures, and by analysing under a special microscope rocks that have been cut into thin, near-transparent sections, they can determine a rock's origin and environment. Sophisticated geochemical analyses can be used to work out the chemical composition of the material.

IGNEOUS ROCKS

In essence, magmas are molten rocks. They vary in original composition – some are acidic and some are basic. Magmas rise towards the surface of the Earth because they are less dense than the surrounding materials. As they cool and solidify, minerals with a high melting point appear first. Olivine and calcium plagioclase are examples of high-temperature minerals; orthoclase and quartz are formed under lower temperatures. Igneous rocks exhibit a variety of textures which are vital to their description and classification. Those with large, well-formed crystals (phenocrysts) set in a finer groundmass are termed porphyritic, whereas rocks with specific minerals enclosed in larger crystals of another mineral are termed poikilitic or more rarely ophitic.

quartz content	types of feldspar	coarse grained	medium grained	fine grained	general designation
more than 10%	orthoclase and/or sodic plagioclase	**granite**	**microgranite**	**rhyolite**	acidic
little or none		**syenite**	**microsyenite**	**trachyte**	intermediate
	sodi-calcic plagioclase	**diorite**	**microdiorite**	**andesite**	
	calcic plagioclase	**gabbro**	**dolerite**	**basalt**	basic
none	little or no feldspar	**peridotite**			ultrabasic

Classification of igneous rocks.

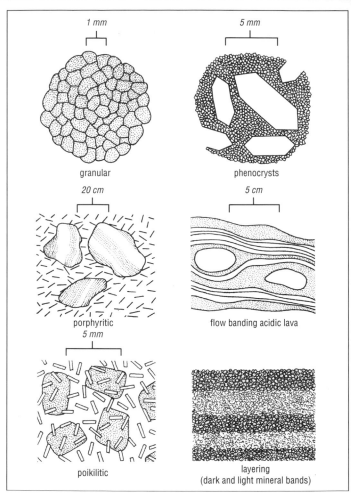

Textures of igneous rocks.

Granite

Type: Acid igneous/magmatic rock.
Grain size: Coarse–very coarse.
Texture: Granular, porphyritic.
Colour: Light, white, grey, pink.
Appearance and rock facts: Granites are usually pale-coloured, acid igneous rocks. The colour is caused by the presence of light-coloured minerals, such as alkali feldspar and quartz. The amount of visible quartz must be greater than 10 per cent for the rock to be classified as a granite. Dark minerals, such as biotite and hornblende, occur in lower percentages, giving the rock a speckled appearance. Granites are coarse to very coarse grained, with crystals of feldspar growing to as much as 8–10 centimetres in length. Granites occur throughout the world, and are among the most common igneous rocks. They are used as a source of aggregates, as ornamental stone, and may also be the host to minerals such as copper and tin. Excellent exposures of granite may be seen in Devon, Cornwall, and the English Lake District.

Granite Pegmatite

Type: Acid igneous/magmatic rock.
Grain size: Coarse–very coarse.
Texture: Granular, coarsely porphyritic.
Colour: White, pink, and red.
Appearance and rock facts: Granite pegmatites are coarse- to giant-grained igneous rocks. They are white, pink, or red in colour, and often occur in veins. Crystals often grow parallel to one another, and spectacular assemblages of white mica, tourmaline, and beryl can be seen in various field settings. Some crystals 14 metres long have been recorded from rocks of the Black Hills of South Dakota in the United States. Other minerals that occur in granite pegmatites include biotite, corundum, fluorite, topaz, zircon, and sphene. Pegmatites are often found on the margins of granitic intrusions, and tend to represent the last stages of cooling from a magma source.

Syenite

Type: Intermediate igneous/magmatic rock.
Grain size: Coarse.
Texture: Equigranular, porphyritic.
Colour: White, grey, red, pink.
Appearance and rock facts: Syenites are usually red, pink, greyish, or white in colour. They are mostly equigranular, and coarse to very coarse grained. The main

minerals are alkali or sodic feldspars, with quartz reaching 10 per cent or more in quartz syenites. Nepheline syenites are generally lighter in overall colour, with pyroxenes, amphibole, and biotite assuming a greater importance. Syenites are commonly found as dykes, sills, or stocks (intrusion). In contrast to granites, syenites are not common rocks.

67

Diorite

Type: Intermediate igneous/magmatic rock.
Grain size: Coarse.
Texture: Equigranular, porphyritic.
Colour: Speckled, black and white, green, pink.
Appearance and rock facts: Diorites are coarse-grained to pegmatitic intermediate igneous rocks. They have little or no visible quartz, and their mineralogy is dominated by plagioclase feldspars and hornblende. Subsidiary minerals include biotite and pyroxene. Diorites are darker than granitic rocks, most being speckled black and white or dark green and even pink. They can be equigranular or porphyritic (conspicuous crystals floating in a fine-grained or glassy ground mass). Diorites occur as intrusions (stocks and bosses) and as dykes. They occur at the edges of granite masses, and the two rocks can grade into each other.

Gabbro

Type: Basic igneous/magmatic rock.
Grain size: Coarse–very coarse.
Texture: Granular, porphyritic.
Colour: Grey, dark grey, black.
Appearance and rock facts:
Gabbro is a coarse- to very coarse-grained, basic igneous rock. It contains little or no quartz (except in quartz gabbroic rocks), and the mineralogy is essentially composed of labradorite or bytownite feldspar, pyroxene, olivine, or hornblende. The texture varies from granular to equigranular, but porphyritic gabbro is rare. Grey, dark-grey, and black varieties occur, some with blue or green coloration. Gabbroic rocks may have a layered texture. They occur as stocks, bosses, and dykes, as well as rare sheet-like intrusions or lopoliths. Some of these sheets may extend over several hundred kilometres.

Peridotite

Type: Ultrabasic igneous/magmatic rock.
Grain size: Coarse.
Texture: Granular, sugary.
Colour: Dark green, black.
Appearance and rock facts: Peridotite is an ultrabasic rock. It is medium to coarse grained with a granular texture. Most peridotites are dull green to black in colour. Dark minerals, such as olivine, pyroxene, and hornblende may be associated with biotite and garnet as subsidiary minerals. Quartz is absent, and feldspars are either absent or of minor importance. Peridotite occurs in dykes, sills, and small intrusions. The variety, dunite, has a sugary texture and is usually

lighter in colour. Diamonds are associated with the variety of peridotite called kimberlite that occurs in steeply dipping pipes in South Africa and Russia.

Serpentinite

Type: Secondary ultrabasic igneous rock.
Grain size: Medium–coarse.
Texture: Fractured, waxy, fibrous, blotchy.
Colour: Green, greyish-green, grey-black.
Appearance and rock facts: Serpentinites are derived from rocks that were originally ultrabasic in composition. They are secondary rocks formed through the interaction

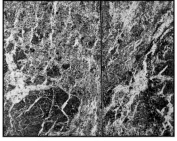

of water and the host rock at low temperatures. Many serpentinites are green or greyish green in colour, highly fractured with veins filled with fibrous serpentine minerals. Bright-green varieties are prized as ornamental or facing stones in the construction industry. Apart from serpentine, olivine, pyroxene, mica, garnet, and iron oxides are found in these rocks. Serpentinites occur as dykes or as lenses in metamorphic areas. The process by which the primary ferro-magnesian minerals are converted to serpentine minerals is termed serpentinization.

Kimberlite

Type: Ultrabasic igneous/magmatic rock.
Grain size: Coarse.
Texture: Porphyritic.
Colour: Dark green, blue-black.
Appearance and rock facts: Kimberlites are uncommon in many parts of the world. They occur in steeply dipping pipes or as dykes, and are associated with diamond exploration. Olivine, micas, and garnets such as pyrope are the most abundant minerals, with pyroxenes, chromite, and ilmenite as subsidiary grains. The texture is usually porphyritic but can appear granular due to the fragmentation of specific crystals. Kimberlites are frequently serpentinized, with a pervasive dark-green coloration. In the field kimberlite pipes are normally 100–300 metres across. Kimberlite dykes are less commonly known.

Micritegranite

Type: Acid igneous/magmatic rock.
Grain size: Medium.
Texture: Granular, porphyritic.
Colour: Light, white, grey, pink, speckled.
Appearance and rock facts: Microgranites are medium-grained, acid igneous rocks. They have more than 10 per cent visible quartz, and are light coloured. Grey-coloured rocks are commonplace, but yellowish and red-pink varieties are also recorded locally. Crystals of quartz and pale-coloured feldspars are common, with biotite and hornblende as subsidiary minerals. It is difficult to determine the composition of the groundmass without a hand lens or a thin section. Microgranites occur as dykes or sills, and commonly cut through granites and finer-grained veins. Microgranites occur in Devon, Cornwall, the English Lake District, and Scotland.

Microdiorite

Type: Intermediate igneous/magmatic rock
Grain size: Medium.
Texture: Porphyritic.
Colour: Grey–dark grey.
Appearance and rock facts: Microdiorites occur at the more basic end of the intermediate group of igneous rocks. Quartz is largely absent, and the main minerals are hornblende, biotite, and sometimes augite. The texture is usually porphyritic with light- and dark-coloured crystals standing out against a grey to dark-grey groundmass. Green and pink varieties of microdiorite exist. Microdiorites occur as dykes and sills, and several dyke swarms are composed of this medium-grained rock. The swarms tend to run across country in a parallel to sub-parallel manner linked to regional fracture patterns.

Dolerite

Type: Basic igneous/magmatic/volcanic rock.
Grain size: Medium.
Texture: Equigranular, ophitic, porphyritic.
Colour: Dark grey, green.
Appearance and rock facts: Dolerite is an example of a medium-grained, basic igneous rock. It is also known as diabase. Texturally, dolerites may be equigranular or ophitic with small crystals enclosed by larger ones. The crystals represent olivine, pyroxene, and plagioclase, with rarer quartz and biotite in the groundmass. Vesicles and amygdales may be present, lined or filled with more exotic minerals. Dolerites are dark grey to black, green, or mottled black and white. They occur as dykes and sills, and are commonly found in dyke swarms. Dolerites are known from North Wales, the English Lake District, and Scotland.

Rhyolite

Type: Acid igneous/volcanic rock.
Grain size: Fine.
Texture: Granular, porphyritic.
Colour: Light, white, grey, pink.
Appearance and rock facts: Rhyolites are light-coloured, fine- to very fine-grained igneous rocks that occur as flows, dykes, and plugs. The parent magma is viscous to highly viscous, with only a limited potential to flow very far. White, grey, green, red-brown, evenly coloured or banded varieties are recorded from around the world. Individual crystals are difficult to see but exotic minerals may occur in vugs and amygdales, and spherules filled with radiating needles of quartz or feldspar can occur. These three structures, essentially holes, are usually formed by escaping gases. Rhyolites are composed of feldspar, quartz, hornblende, and mica. Flow-banded rhyolites are commonplace in North Wales, the English Lake District, and parts of Scotland.

Trachyte

Type: Intermediate igneous/volcanic rock.
Grain size: Fine.
Texture: Porphyritic.
Colour: White, grey, pink.
Appearance and rock facts: Trachytes are intermediate, fine-grained igneous rocks. They are slightly darker than rhyolites, and are mostly grey with white and pink varieties. Crystals of feldspar (sanidine) 'float' in a fine-grained matrix. There is less than 10 per cent quartz, and both matrix and crystals are mainly alkali feldspar. Aegirine (pyroxene) and hornblende may occur but only in small percentages. Trachytes occur as dykes, sills, and flows. They form from acid lavas, and can have a glassy, rubbly appearance at the edge of a viscous flow.

Andesite

Type: Intermediate igneous/volcanic rock.
Grain size: Fine.
Texture: Porphyritic.
Colour: Dark, grey-black.
Appearance and rock facts: Andesitic rocks are more basic than trachytes. They are fine grained but darker in colour, with grey to black, green, purple, and brown varieties commonplace. Texturally, they are mostly porphyritic, with plagioclase feldspar crystals set in a feldspar-rich groundmass. Dark mica (biotite), hornblende, or augite may occur as subsidiary minerals. These minerals can be seen with the naked eye or with a hand lens. Andesites exhibit flow structures, and vugs, vesicles, and amygdales are characteristic. Basic magmas spread out across country in a sheet-like manner. Andesites and basalts develop crusts with ropy or cindery surfaces. Pillow structures occur when hot, basic magmas are spilled on to the sea-floor.

Basalt

Type: Basic igneous/volcanic rock.
Grain size: Fine.
Texture: Dense, porphyritic.
Colour: Black, grey black.
Appearance and rock facts: Basalts are perhaps the best-known, fine-grained igneous rocks. They are black or grey-black in colour, with olivine, pyroxene, and white-grey feldspars as the larger crystals. The texture varies, but it is usually difficult to identify individual minerals in hand specimen.

Basalts are often vesicular or amygdaloidal, with these cavities filled with accessory minerals, including zeolites. Basalts form from basic magmas; they form sheet-like bodies over large areas, and may cool to form the classic hexagonal columns seen in the Giant's Causeway, Northern Ireland. Basalts also occur as dykes or sills, and can have a glassy appearance. Ropy (pahoehoe) and cindery or blocky (aa) surfaces are typical in these igneous rocks.

Agglomerate

Type: Volcanic rock.
Grain size: Coarse.
Texture: Fragmental, welded.
Colour: Varied.
Appearance and rock facts: Agglomerates are fragmental volcanic rocks associated with craters and the sides of volcanic cones. The fragments are poorly sorted, and range from 64 millimetres to 30 centimetres (plus or minus) in size. Most are angular, but rounded or spindle-shaped bombs, with internal vesicles, are commonplace. The constituent materials reflect the original composition of the parent magma, and agglomerates form in areas characterized by basaltic or andesitic flows. Ancient vent agglomerates, found in North Wales or Scotland, are consolidated, while those from the Puy area of France, deposited over the last 10,000 to 1 million years, are rubbly in appearance.

Tuff

Type: Volcanic rock.
Grain size: Fine–coarse.
Texture: Granular, fragmental, glassy.
Colour: Grey, buff, mottled.
Appearance and rock facts: Tuffaceous rocks are essentially finer-grained, fragmental volcanic rocks. Grain size should not exceed 64 millimetres. They are the consolidated or welded equivalent of ashes. Lithic tuffs are composed of

crystalline rock fragments, vitric tuffs of pumice grains, and crystal tuffs of mineral clasts. It is likely that all three varieties will occur in the immediate vicinity of a volcanic crater. Some volcanic fragments found in tuffs are termed lapilli; these are typically rounded or ellipsoidal in shape. They represent small pieces of molten lava that are ejected during a violent eruption.

Ash

Type: Volcanic rock.
Grain size: Fine–medium grained.
Texture: Granular.
Colour: White, grey, buff, yellow.
Appearance and rock facts: Essentially, ash is a descriptive term for finer-grained, unconsolidated, fragmental volcanic rocks. They are often light coloured and, like tuffs, can be layered or show grading. Heavy rainfall or deposition in water can result in flow structures. Several

types of ash are known, and the terms are applied to describe texture and composition. Ashes are expelled from volcanic craters in great clouds; they can cover vast areas and easily destroy all forms of life over hundreds of square kilometres. Recent examples of violent volcanic activity that have produced huge amounts of ash and tuffaceous materials are Mount Pinaturbo in the Far East and Montserrat in the Caribbean.

Ignimbrite

Type: Volcanic rock.
Grain size: Fine–coarse grained.
Texture: Granular–glassy.
Colour: Speckled, white, yellow, buff.

Appearance and rock facts: Ignimbrites are composed of fragments of volcanic pumice, a highly vesicular glass. The fragments are usually less than 1 centimetre in size, flattened, and angular in shape. Ignimbrites have a similar composition to rhyolites and trachytes, which are fine-grained acidic and intermediate lavas. They are essentially hot volcanic ash which is ejected rapidly, retaining heat, large amounts of gas, and red-hot fragments. They are deposited over the slopes of the parent volcano but gravity enhances their ability to flow, and many ignimbrites are layered. They may cool to form columnar joints.

Obsidian/Pitchstone

Type: Volcanic rock.
Grain size: Glassy.
Texture: Vitreous, microcrystalline.
Colour: Black, brown.

Appearance and rock facts: Obsidian and pitchstone occur in dykes and lava flows. They have the same composition as rhyolite, and are essentially volcanic glass. Pitchstone may have relatively large crystals of quartz or feldspar 'floating' in a very fine-grained matrix, but this is unusual in obsidian. Obsidian is much shinier than pitchstone, with black, brown, and grey varieties to be seen in the field. Both are siliceous and break with a conchoidal fracture. Aboriginal peoples used obsidian to make arrow- and spear-heads. They knapped the stone, using the conchoidal fracture to trim fine pieces away from the original specimen. Well-shaped, exceptionally sharp weapons were the reward for their labours.

Pumice

Type: Volcanic rock.
Grain size: Fine grained.
Texture: Vesicular.
Colour: White–grey.
Appearance and rock facts: Pumice is simply a rhyolite with myriads of vesicles or holes, giving it a sponge-like texture. It is formed during the initial, gas-rich phases of a volcanic eruption when the density of the original magma is greatly reduced by the presence of gas bubbles. Pumice is usually white or grey, and glass rich. Shades of yellow, red, and green are known. The vesicles may be filled with late-stage minerals such as zeolites, and quartz and feldspar crystals may exist within the frothy groundmass. Pumice is known throughout the world, and is used as an abrasive and in the cosmetics industry.

Volcanic Bombs

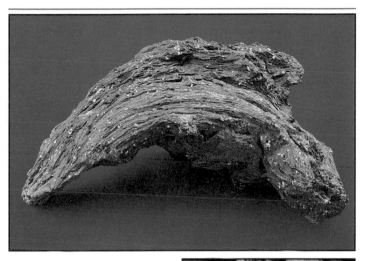

Type: Intermediate–basic volcanic.
Grain size: Large–very large, rounded, spindle shaped.
Texture: Glassy, rough exterior.
Colour: Brown–grey-black.
Appearance and rock facts: Volcanic bombs reflect the composition of the parent magma. They are ejecta, thrown out during violent, explosive volcanic activity. Lumps of molten lava are thrown into the air, and transport and cooling

result in rounded, ellipsoidal, and spindle-shaped exotics. Bombs are usually associated with intermediate and basic lavas such as andesite and basalt. Reheated and fragmented country rocks, ripped from the inside of a volcano, can be included in the vast amount of material thrown out during an explosive episode. These bombs are of mixed composition and are cracked across their outer surfaces.

SEDIMENTARY ROCKS

Sedimentary rocks are divided into two major groups, clastics and carbonates. Clastic rocks, such as sandstones and grits, are essentially fragmental; and the grains or fragments are produced by mechanical or chemical processes. Weathering encompasses many of these processes of disintegration and decomposition. Carbonate rocks, including limestones and evaporites, are produced through chemical–organic processes, with the precipitation of minerals and the growth of animal and plant skeletons controlled, in part, by temperature and salinity. Clastic rocks can be classified by grain size, carbonates on the basis of their mud content and origin

Conglomerate

Type: Clastic/rudaceous.
Grain size: Coarse–very coarse.
Grain type: Boulders, cobbles, pebbles.
Colour: Variable.
Appearance and rock facts: Conglomerates are rudaceous clastic sediments in which the grains are larger than 2 millimetres in size. The range of material is important in their description, with boulders, cobbles, and pebbles often sourced from different rock types. Pebbles: 2–64 millimetres; cobbles 64–256 millimetres; boulders 256 milimetres or larger. These may be set in a fine- to medium-grained matrix with more ancient rocks consolidated or cemented. They accumulate in shallow-water environments such as rivers and coastal waters. They are the product of weathering and transport.

Breccia

Type: Clastic/rudaceous.
Grain size: Coarse–very coarse.
Grain type: Angular grains.
Colour: Variable.
Appearance and rock facts: Unlike conglomerates, breccias are composed of angular grains or fragments. These range from 2 millimetres to metres in size, and are frequently found on scree slopes in glaciated or arid areas. They are often

the product of *in situ* weathering and limited transport. Bedding is not as marked as it is in conglomerates although the tile-like stacking of fragments (imbrication) and structures within a matrix serve as indicators of the direction of movement. The environment of deposition does not support plant or animal life, and fossils are inevitably rare. Reworked brecciated material can occur in shallow-water environments. Fault breccias are composed of fragments of the faulted rock often set in a calcite or quartz cement.

Till/Tillite

Type: Clastic/glacial.
Grain size: Coarse–very coarse. Clay or sandy clay matrix
Grain type: Angular–rounded fragments.
Colour: Brown, grey, green.
Appearance and rock facts: Glacial tills are formed by the action of glaciers. They are unsorted, and large blocks and boulders may be set in a fine to medium, clay-rich matrix. Bedding is absent although the alignment of specific fragments may indicate direction of movement. Tills are also known as boulder clays. They can cover vast areas. Tillite is the name given to fossil till deposits, and the oldest examples are known from the Precambrian Era. Tillites are invariably consolidated and cemented; in ancient areas, they may also be metamorphosed.

Sandstone

Type: Clastic/arenaceous.
Grain size: Very fine–coarse.
Grain type: Granular.
Colour: Variable.
Appearance and rock facts: Sands and sandstones are described in terms of their mineralogy and grain size. Grains may be sourced from a variety of materials but range in size from $\frac{1}{16}$–2 millimetres in diameter. They may be angular to rounded, poorly sorted to well sorted, cemented or uncemented, and poorly to well bedded. Quartz is the main constituent of many sandstones, with feldspar, mica, glauconite, phosphates, and other subsidiary minerals. Orthoquartzites are composed of quartz grains in a quartz cement. Cements also vary with the environment of deposition and post-burial processes. Siliceous, calcareous, and ferruginous cements are commonplace. Sandstones are the products of weathering and erosion, and are formed in rivers, on the continental platform, and in desert environments.

Arkose

Type: Clastic/arenaceous.
Grain size: Medium–coarse.
Grain type: Granular.
Colour: Grey, pink, red.
Appearance and rock facts: Arkoses
are sandstones with high percentages of
feldspars (25–50 per cent). Grains are
fairly rounded and only moderately
sorted. Apart from feldspar, quartz is

present in large amounts, with the micas as subsidiary minerals. These are
usually found in calcite or iron oxide cements. In the field, arkoses are generally
poorly to crudely bedded with poorly defined cross-bedding. They are
frequently found in association with conglomeratic materials. The two may
interdigitate, with the arkoses forming thick wedges within the sequence. This
association suggests that deposition was rapid and that it took place close to the
source of the constituent minerals. Feldspars and micas do not travel far before
disintegrating, and most arkoses are deposited in interior basins proximal to
exposed igneous rocks.

Greywacke

Type: Clastic/arenaceous.
Grain size: Fine–coarse.
Grain type: Granular.
Colour: Grey, green, black.
Appearance and rock facts:
Greywackes are deposited in relatively
deep-water marine environments beyond
the continental shelf. They are associated
with rapid subsidence of the basin, and
are deposited as turbidity currents. The
latter are triggered by earthquakes or by
instability within an accumulation of

sediment at the top of the continental shelf. The downslope movement of the
sediment mass or slurry is spectacular. Thick turbidite sequences exhibit graded
bedding (coarse base, fine top). The grains are mostly subangular to angular, and
set in an argillaceous (clay-rich) matrix. Quartz, feldspar, and rock fragments are
the main constituents of these rock types.

Grit/Gravel

Type: Clastic/arenaceous.
Grain size: Medium–coarse.
Grain type: Granular.
Colour: Variable.
Appearance and rock facts: Grits and gravels are terms used to describe specific types of arenaceous rocks which are often unconsolidated. Grits are composed of angular fragments. The sharp edges to individual grains indicate an immature, medium- to coarse-grained sandstone that has not been transported over a great distance. The grains are usually dominated by quartz. Gravels are essentially river deposits with grains ranging from 2 to 4 millimetres in size. They are largely rudaceous rocks deposited in a high-energy environment. The grains are usually subrounded to rounded, and the percentage of matrix is variable. Fossil mammals, such as deer, horses, and rhinos, are often found in ancient river gravels of the Thames Estuary.

Siltstone

Type: Clastic/argillaceous.
Grain size: Fine.
Grain type: Laminated.
Colour: White, grey, buff, yellow.
Appearance and rock facts: Silts and siltstones are defined on grain size. Individual grains range from $\frac{1}{16}$ to $\frac{1}{256}$ millimetre in size, and the larger grains are mainly quartz or feldspar. Flakes of claystones and minute fragments of plant material can also occur locally, depending upon the environment of deposition. Most siltstones have a clay matrix but some can be washed and almost clay free. Mica may commonly occur as a subsidiary mineral, micaceous siltstones having a distinct surface sheen. Siltstones may exhibit a fine-scale lamination, ripples, and cross-lamination. They are widely distributed. Marine, lacustrine, and glacial silts and siltstones are well documented in the geological record.

Mudstone

Type: Clastic/argillaceous.
Grain size: Very fine
Grain type: Clay-rich, calcareous.
Colour: Variable.
Appearance and rock facts: Muds and clays are essentially unconsolidated or non-compacted mudstones and claystones. In terms of grain size, all are argillaceous (⅟₁₆ millimetre or finer), but mudstones and claystones (and their unconsolidated equivalents) differ in their clay content. Mudstones are largely very fine-grained carbonates which react with dilute hydrochloric acid. They can be fossiliferous, and are often produced by the break-up of plant and animal skeletons. Claystones are composed of clay minerals with quartz, feldspar, and mica as minor components. Mudstones and claystones are associated with low-energy environments such as lakes and quiescent marine conditions. The Tertiary clays of southern England are often rich in fossils.

Shale

Type: Clastic/argillaceous.
Grain size: Very fine.
Grain type: Laminated; fissile–sub-fissile.
Colour:
Appearance and rock facts: Shales are compacted clays that tend to split readily into thin layers (fissile). They are composed of clay minerals but are often rich in organic matter. Black shales, identical to those in the Kimmeridge Clay sequence along the Dorset coast, are the major source rocks for the North Sea oil fields. They were deposited in a marine environment rich in planktonic (free-floating) microscopic plants and animals with common or even abundant communities of bivalves and trace fossils. Black shales are often pyritized, with pyritic crystals, or framboids, scattered within the matrix. Pyritized ammonites and bivalves are locally abundant in the Jurassic shales of Somerset and Yorkshire.

Carbonate rocks also range in grain size but they are normally classified in terms of their mud content and their origin. Organic carbonates, such as shelly limestones or chalk, are formed from the skeletal remains of plants and animals, whereas evaporitic carbonates are the products of chemical processes such as precipitation.

Bioclastic/Shelly Limestone

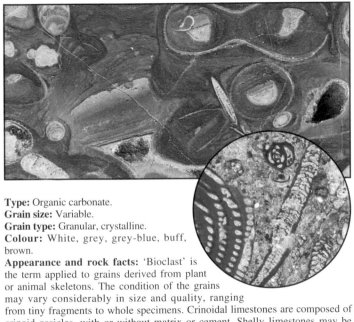

Type: Organic carbonate.
Grain size: Variable.
Grain type: Granular, crystalline.
Colour: White, grey, grey-blue, buff, brown.
Appearance and rock facts: 'Bioclast' is the term applied to grains derived from plant or animal skeletons. The condition of the grains may vary considerably in size and quality, ranging from tiny fragments to whole specimens. Crinoidal limestones are composed of crinoid ossicles, with or without matrix or cement. Shelly limestones may be fragmental or packed with the shells of a single species set in a mud matrix. Recrystallization is commonplace in bioclastic limestones, with coarse, blocky calcite replacing the original structure. Chalcedonic silica may also occur as a mineral. Limestones vary greatly in grain size and composition. Mud-rich limestones are termed mudstones and wackestones; limestones with less than 10 per cent matrix are either packstones or wackestones. Framestones and bindstones are associated with reef-building organisms such as corals.

Chalk

Type: Organic carbonate.
Grain size: Very fine grained.
Grain type: Chalky, friable, compact
Colour: White, grey, yellowish.
Appearance and rock facts: Chalk is mainly white, bedded, and often packed with cherts and flint nodules. A closer look reveals that many chalks are pure limestones packed with the skeletons of microscopic organisms such as coccoliths and planktonic foraminiferids. The presence of mud or clay can give chalk a wispy or mottled appearance, and even a greenish coloration. Chalks are usually deposited in deep marine environments beyond the continental shelf. Ammonites, bivalves, echinoids, and trace fossils are locally abundant in chalk sequences. Marcasite nodules are also easy to find. Chalk rocks crop out extensively along the coastlines of south-east England and Yorkshire.

Oolitic Limestone

Type: Organic carbonate.
Grain size: Fine–medium.
Grain type: Rounded, roe-like grains; bioclastic.
Colour: White, buff, yellow, grey-brown.
Appearance and rock facts: Oolitic limestones are associated with warm, shallow-water marine environments. Oolitic shoals exist today in the Bahamas. Ooids are rounded grains of carbonate accreted around a mineral or organic nucleus. They rarely exceed 2 millimetres in size, and most oolitic rocks are composed of 1-millimetre grains. Fossils are common to abundant, although many of those found in ancient oolitic limestones are probably derived. Oolitic shoals are mobile sea-floor sediments; they are not conducive to the growth of plant colonies, and the fauna is dominated by free-swimming and bottom-crawling organisms.

Lumachelle/Coquina

Type: Organic carbonate.
Grain size: Variable.
Grain type: Shells.
Colour: Variable.
Appearance and rock facts:
Lumachellic limestones and coquinas
are usually composed of bivalve or
gastropod shells, and the organisms
are often found in life position.
Oysters are commonly found in great

numbers in Tertiary sediments with myriad valves and articulated shells associated
with a limited amount of mud or clay matrix. Shells can be transported short
distances to form shell banks in river estuaries or as beach deposits. Rudist bivalves
built large, 'reef-like' mounds during the Mesozoic Era.

Dolomite

Type: Chemical carbonate.
Grain size: Very fine–coarsely
crystalline.
Grain type: Crystalline–sugary.
Colour: Yellow, buff, brown, orange-
brown, white, grey.
Appearance and rock facts: The
term 'dolomite' is used to describe
both the mineral and a range of rock
types. The rocks can be composed of
aggregates of well-formed (euhedral)

rhombs, or granular aggregates in which the crystals interlock to form a distinctive
mosaic. Dolomite may occur as a very early to late replacement mineral during the
burial and chemical alteration of carbonate rocks. In areas of carbonate
precipitation, dolomite may occur as a primary deposit. Dolomitization of a
carbonate rock can attain many levels, with the final result being the destruction of
the constituent grains (bioclasts, ooids, etc.) and the recrystallization of the matrix.
Dolomites may be more porous than the equivalent limestone owing to the change
from calcium carbonate to magnesium carbonate. The solution of skeletal material
can result in vugs and moulds. Dolomites are seen as potential reservoir rocks in
petroleum exploration.

Travertine/Tufa

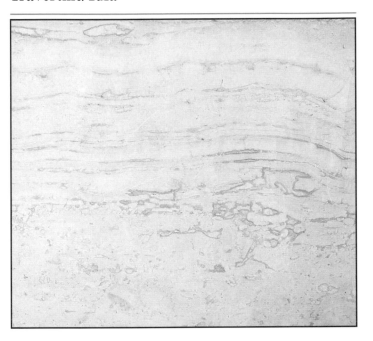

Type: Chemical carbonate.
Grain size: Stalactitic, massive.
Grain type: Fibrous, porous, spongy.
Colour: White, yellow, orange-brown, red.
Appearance and rock facts: Travertine is a calcium carbonate rock deposited by precipitation from carbonate-rich waters in caves or around hot springs. The rate of precipitation varies depending upon the water saturation and temperature. In caves, stalactites and stalagmites are usually massive with a fibrous internal structure. Hot-spring deposits tend to be layered, concentric, spherical, or rounded. Tufa, or calc-sinter, is a spongy form of travertine. Plant remains and gastropod shells can be found in association with these deposits. Calc-tufa can also be found as a fissure or fracture fill-in in limestone areas.

Rock Salt/Halite

Type: Precipitate/evaporite.
Grain size: Crystals 1 mm–1 cm.
Grain type: Crystalline–sugary.
Colour: Colourless, white, orange, purple, yellow-brown.
Appearance and rock facts: Rock salt (halite) is formed from the evaporation of sea brines. This usually takes place in coastal sabkha environments such as those along the North African coast or in the Middle East. It occurs as bedded units with shale partings. Sedimentary structures are absent, but rock salt is readily contorted during compaction or flow. Beds of rock salt are usually massive and coarsely crystalline. Perfect individual crystals can occur, especially as linings to arched structures (tepees) formed as the desiccation of the sabkha surface take place. Halite is the major source of table salt. Although it is soluble, it persists in sedimentary sequences where it is overlain by an impervious claystone.

Gypsum

Type: Precipitate/evaporite ($CaSO_4.2H_2O$).
Grain size: Variable.
Grain type: Nodular, massive, crystalline, fibrous.
Colour: Colourless, white, orange, purple, yellow-brown.
Appearance and rock facts: Nodules and beds of gypsum are frequently encountered in sedimentary sequences deposited in sabkha or hypersaline basins. Gypsum is very insoluble, and is one of the first minerals to be precipitated in such environments. It is usually associated with halite and anhydrite, and may be interbedded with thin shales, soils, and gastropodal limestones. Gypsum may also occur as a replacement for anhydrite through the process of hydration (addition of water). Fibrous gypsum is called satin spar, whereas selenite is the name given to a transparent variety often found as well-formed crystals in clays.

Ironstone

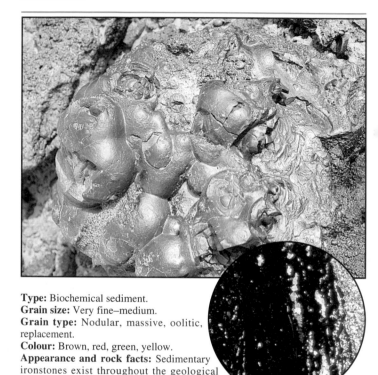

Type: Biochemical sediment.
Grain size: Very fine–medium.
Grain type: Nodular, massive, oolitic, replacement.
Colour: Brown, red, green, yellow.
Appearance and rock facts: Sedimentary ironstones exist throughout the geological record. They can be formed in several ways, but typically contain more than 15 per cent iron. Oolitic ironstones form in shallow-water environments from iron-aluminium-rich gels. On burial the original materials are converted to chamosite (oxidized chloritic mineral). Iron nodules (siderite) can develop in claystone sequences, and haematite, siderite, and chamosite can occur as replacement minerals in carbonate rocks. Many economic iron ores are chemical precipitates. Black-band ironstones are a mixture of iron carbonate and carbonaceous material, whereas bog iron is a product of bacterial activity in peat bogs.

Bauxite (Aluminium-rich Laterite)

Type: Chemically enriched deposit.
Grain size: Medium–coarse.
Grain type: Oolitic–pisolitic.
Colour: Yellow-brown, reddish, grey.
Appearance and rock facts: Bauxite is essentially a mineral-enriched deposit produced by the weathering of rocks rich in aluminium. It is a mixture of aluminium oxides and hydroxides, with iron oxides, silica, and titanium among the major impurities. Bauxite is the main source of aluminium. It is formed in tropical and subtropical environments where the original rocks are subjected to prolonged weathering and leaching. Such deposits are termed laterites. The overall effect is to reduce the percentage of the silica in the rock. Bauxite may be earthy, oolitic, or pisolitic in habit. Commercial discoveries contain 20–30 per cent aluminium.

Phosphorite/Phosphate Rock

Type: Biochemical.
Grain size: Fine–coarse.
Grain type: Granular, nodular, oolitic, pelloidal.
Colour: White, brown, buff, yellow, black.
Appearance and rock facts: Phosphorites are distributed throughout the world. They are often associated with glauconitic sediments, and may contain a high percentage of glauconite. Most phosphorites are reworked, although deposition is usually associated with a slow rate of sedimentation on the outer continental shelf. Exceptions to this do exist, however, and some Tunisian phosphates, for example, are interbedded with shoreline sediments. High percentages of collophane (apatite) characterize phosphatic deposits. It can occur as ooids or pellets, and as the remains of vertebrate organisms. Phosphate nodules form by chemical precipitation, and lenses of such nodules are found in the Gault Clay of southern England. Guano (bird droppings) is a rich source of phosphate which is mined on oceanic islands.

Paramoudra

Type: Chemical sediment.
Grain size: Very fine–medium fine.
Form: Irregular, nodular, dense.
Colour: Brown, yellow-brown, black.
Appearance and rock facts: Paramoudra are commonly associated with clay-rich sandstones, sandstones, and alternating sandstone–claystone sequences. Excellent examples occur frequently on the north-east coast of England, in Jurassic sediments. They are usually hard and fine to medium grained with a sandy texture. They may often be large to very large in size, irregular in shape with a low, broad profile. The majority of samples occur parallel to the bedding of the sediments in which they are enclosed. Paramoudra are thought to be the product of post-burial chemical activity within the sediment, but their origins are still the subject of considerable debate.

Flint Nodules

Type: Chemical sediment.
Grain size: Very fine.
Grain type: Nodular, dense.
Colour: Brown, blue-grey, black.
Appearance and rock facts: Flint nodules are commonly found in chalk deposits throughout England. A nodule has a white, chalky external covering but internally it is hard and very fine grained with a vitreous sheen. Flint nodules break with a conchoidal fracture often revealing a hollow centre or a fossil as a nucleus. Neither chert nor flint has a crystalline structure and it is very difficult to distinguish between them. Chert is often associated with older limestones such as those of the Carboniferous Period. Flint nodules were extensively used as a building material, particularly in the construction of churches in the south of England. Siliceous nodules are associated with either volcanic activity or with the dissolution of siliceous sponges.

METAMORPHIC ROCKS

Metamorphic rocks are essentially mineral aggregates formed by the recrystallization of country rocks as a result of changes in temperature, pressure, or the percentage of volatiles (water, carbon dioxide, sulphur dioxide etc.). Metamorphism is the process of change, with new mineral phases accompanying changes in texture and fabric. It can occur on a local or regional scale. Localized metamorphism may be associated with the emplacement of basic or acidic magmas, resulting in the baking of nearby rocks. Impact metamorphism caused by a meteorite landing is also localized, as are the effects of faulting (mylonites, platy streaked rocks). Regional metamorphism is usually associated with mountain building, when significant changes in temperature and pressure occur at several layers within the Earth's crust and mantle. Rocks can descend by as much as 30 kilometres in these orogenic belts, and temperatures can rise to 800 °C. Thick sedimentary sequences are associated with these terrains while igneous intrusions are emplaced during the development of folded mountain chains. Water from the sediments and heat from the magmatic rocks promote further changes in mineralization.

By contrast, burial metamorphism is a low-temperature, high-pressure process which occurs at the base of thick sedimentary sequences in large-scale basins. The mineral assemblages are typically low-temperature types, and recrystallization is incomplete.

Slate

Type/occurrence: Metamorphic aureole around igneous intrusion.
Grain size: Fine.
Texture Argillaceous; flat platy cleavage.
Colour: Grey, green, purple, black.
Appearance and rock facts: Slates are invariably dark- to darkish-coloured rocks characterized by a

distinct platy cleavage. They are very fine grained, originating from the contact metamorphism of argillaceous or pelitic rocks. The texture is usually homogeneous but spotted slates are commonplace. The spots are rounded or spherical in shape, and can be deformed subsequently by regional pressure. Spots may be graphite rich. Slates may also contain crystals of andalusite, and may grade laterally into hornfels. Slates are also associated with regional metamorphism.

Hornfels

Type/occurrence: Contact metamorphic rock associated with igneous intrusions.
Grain size: Fine–fine-medium.
Texture Homogeneous, equigranular, porphyroblastic.
Colour: Grey, green, blue, black.
Appearance and rock facts: Hornfelses are usually coarser grained than slates. They tend to splinter rather than cleave, and are noted for the presence of large, well-developed crystals (porphyroblasts) of andalusite and cordierite. Mineral fragments, or porphyroclasts, also occur. Andalusite occurs as rectangular prisms, and cordierite as rounded grains. Cross-shaped crystals of andalusite (chiastolite) are found locally. Andalusite hornfeles may originate very near to, or actually in contact with, an igneous intrusion.

Marble

Type/occurrence: Contact metamorphism of limestones.
Grain size: Medium–coarse.
Texture Granular, sugary.
Colour: White, grey, green, black, red.
Appearance and rock facts: Marble is produced by the metamorphism of limestones by igneous intrusions. They can grade into metamorphosed carbonates and may be interbedded with hornfelses. Marbles are composed of calcium carbonate but subsidiary minerals, such as olivine, serpentine, and tremolite do occur. Depending upon the grade of metamorphism, original structures and even fossils may persist and add to the quality of the rock. For the construction industry, dating back to Roman times, the most famous and prized rocks are the pure-white and banded marbles quarried in Italy. This Carrara marble was extensively used by the Italian sculptor, painter, architect, Michelangelo (1475–1564).

Skarn

Type/occurrence: Metamorphic rock associated with diorite, granite, and syenite intrusions.
Grain size: Fine–coarse.
Texture: Crystalline, layered, nodular, massive.
Colour: Variable, grey, brown, black.
Appearance and rock facts: Skarn is composed of calcium silicates, with considerable amounts of iron, aluminium, and magnesium. The grain size of skarns varies but can appear very coarse because of the development of garnets, and economic accumulations of magnetite and copper sulphides. The silicon, iron, aluminium, and magnesium minerals are sourced from the nearby granite, diorite, or syenite intrusions. The original country rocks are limestones or dolomites. Skarns tend to interdigitate with the limestone rocks.

Phyllite

Type/occurrence: Low-grade regional metamorphic rock.
Grain size: Fine–medium.
Texture Schistose, micaceous, chloritic, foliated.
Colour: Green, grey.
Appearance and rock facts: Phyllites are formed by the low-grade metamorphism of argillaceous or pelitic rocks. They can occur over large areas and grade into higher-grade metamorphic rocks such as schists. Phyllites exhibit a well-developed schistosity, a pronounced fabric which results from the parallel alignment of platy minerals such as chlorite, muscovite, and sericite. Such rocks have a silky sheen and split easily. They do not cleave as easily as slates, however, and are less extensively used as roof tiles. Phyllites are widespread in folded mountain belts.

Schist

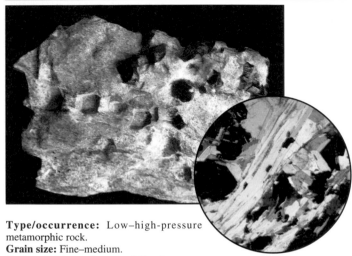

Type/occurrence: Low–high-pressure metamorphic rock.
Grain size: Fine–medium.
Texture Schistose, lustrous, foliated.
Colour: Green, bluish purple, black.
Appearance and rock facts: Schists are regional metamorphic rocks formed by the alteration of pelitic and argillaceous rocks. They are coarser grained than phyllites, with individual grains larger than 1 millimetre in size. Several major types of schist can be seen in areas of regional metamorphism. Their texture and overall mineralogy vary in relation to the degree of metamorphism. Low-grade metamorphism can result in the development of chloritic schists in which the mineral chlorite is a major constituent. It is flaky or clotted but not easily seen with the naked eye. The green or greyish colours of these rocks are due to the presence of chlorite. Sericite and muscovite schists occur in zones of moderate metamorphism. They have a well-developed schistosity, and the flaky minerals give a bright, lustrous appearance. Biotite schists, garnetiferous and glaucophane schists are associated with high-pressure regimes. Their grain size and mineralogy may vary but the prefix to the overall name describes the most important component. Schists are often folded, and may exhibit mineral segregation and layering. Kyanite and sillimanite schists occur in the highest-grade zones of metamorphism. They are often found in association with granites and migmatites.

Granulite

Type/occurrence: High-temperature, high-pressure metamorphic rock.
Grain size: Medium–coarse.
Texture Layered, banded; granular.
Colour: Green, grey.
Appearance and rock facts: Granulites are medium- to coarse-grained metamorphic rocks rich in quartz, feldspar, pyroxene, and garnet. The terms 'basic' and 'acidic' may be applied to granulites with respect to the relative percentages of

their constituents. Granulites are found in areas of high-grade metamorphism. They were probably formed at great depths, and are associated with ancient shield areas that probably originated during the Precambrian Era. Some rocks, termed acid granulites, are also known as charnockitic gneisses. It is often difficult to differentiate between gneisses and granulites in the field.

Eclogite

Type/occurrence: Rare. High-temperature, high-pressure metamorphic rock.
Grain size: Medium–coarse.
Texture Granular, banded.
Colour: Green, red, spotted.
Appearance and rock facts: Eclogites are associated with basic and ultrabasic rocks. They are rare, usually occurring as blocks or lenses in metamorphic and in igneous rocks. The main minerals are pyroxene and

reddish garnets, and more rarely, diamonds. They may be banded and have a granular appearance. Eclogites are dense attractive-looking rocks. It is likely that they are formed as a result of the metamorphism of igneous rocks in the deep crust and upper mantle. High temperatures and huge pressures exist at these depths within the Earth.

Gneiss

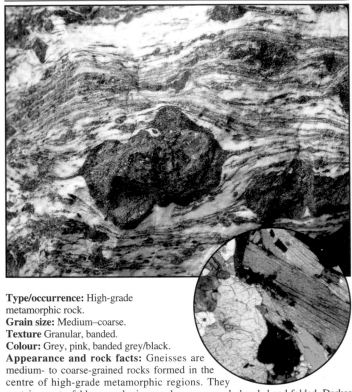

Type/occurrence: High-grade
metamorphic rock.
Grain size: Medium–coarse.
Texture Granular, banded.
Colour: Grey, pink, banded grey/black.
Appearance and rock facts: Gneisses are
medium- to coarse-grained rocks formed in the
centre of high-grade metamorphic regions. They
contain quartz, feldspar, and micas, and are commonly banded and folded. Darker
micaceous minerals tend to alternate with white/pink quartzofeldspathic minerals.
Quartz and coarse pegmatitic veins commonly cut through gneissose rocks in crop
outs. Eye-shaped porphyroblasts of feldspars are common in augen gneisses –
augen meaning 'eyes' in German. Hornblende may occur as a subsidiary mineral
locally. The abundance of a specific mineral may give rise to particular prefixes in
the naming of these rocks, i.e., biotite gneiss or hornblende gneiss.

Migmatite

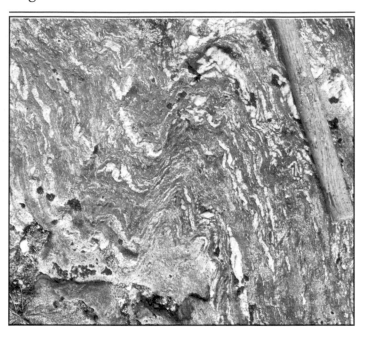

Type/occurrence: High-grade metamorphic rock.
Grain size: Coarse.
Texture Gneissose, foliated, schistose.
Colour: Alternating layers of white, red, black, and grey.
Appearance and rock facts: Migmatites are found in close proximity to granitic intrusions in areas of regional metamorphism. They are often granitic in appearance, with the granitic component entering into the country rock from the granite. The country rock is partially melted and recrystallized, and flow structures become apparent. Texturally, migmatites resemble gneisses but they are usually markedly foliated and may develop a well-defined schistosity. Crystals or porphyroblasts of quartz and feldspar are often present. It is likely that migmatites are formed at depth.

Meteorite

Type/occurrence: Extra-terrestrial iron or stony solid bodies.
Grain size: Fine–coarse.
Texture Dense, fragmental.
Colour: Speckled, brownish.
Appearance and rock facts: Meteorites are divided into three groups depending upon their composition. Most meteorites are composed of silicate minerals with olivine, pyroxene, and plagioclase as the major constituents. Nickel-iron alloys are also abundant in certain meteorites. The largest known meteorites are, in fact, nickel-iron types, with some specimens exceeding 60,000 kilograms in weight. Stony-iron meteorites are mixtures of silicates and nickel-iron, and have well-formed crystals of olivine, pyroxene, and plagioclase present in specific types. Stony meteorites are the most common forms to hit Earth. They have a spherulitic (circular grains) texture, with olivine and pyroxene as the main minerals. Individual stones are often equidimensional.

FOSSILS

Life on Earth began some 3.5 billion years ago. Plants and animals have evolved to occupy a myriad of ecological niches, and different assemblages characterize periods of geological time. The first evidence of life is represented by the stony frameworks associated with simple plants, but the advent of the first community approximately 600 million years ago marked the development of higher groups of animals, and the use of organic materials and minerals as skeletons.

The vast majority of fossils are the hard parts of invertebrate organisms – animals without backbones. These hard parts may be external structures used to support or to protect the organism, or they may be internal skeletons that provide a framework for muscle attachment. Skeletal hard parts developed in single-celled animals and are obvious components of fishes, amphibians, reptiles, birds, and the mammals, including humans. Calcium carbonate, calcium phosphate, and silica are examples of the chemical compounds used in the construction of animal skeletons. Skeletons are more likely to be preserved as fossils than soft tissues. Mineralized skeletons are relatively resistant to scavenging and transportation. Impregnation with minerals carried in fluids passing through a sediment in which they are buried may increase their chances of survival in the fossil record.

Soft tissues, on the other hand, will often decay rapidly, or suffer from scavenging by other animals. Rapid burial in a fine-grained sediment in an anoxic, or oxygen-free, environment will greatly enhance their chance of fossilization. Communities of soft-bodied creatures are preserved throughout the fossil record. But faunas such as those found in the Ediacara Formation of Australia or the Jurassic Solenhofen sediments of Germany represent unique time slices of life on our planet.

Fossil plants are less commonplace than fossil animals, and their preservation also relies on rapid burial in the right kind of sediment. Mineralization of the woody tissues, however, can result in fossils that are resistant to decay and to the ravages of time.

Myriads of animals move freely across the ocean floors, or burrow or bore into the substrate in search of food or protection. Land-dwellers also create burrows or hiding places, and walk or crawl between feeding or resting sites. The tracks and trails, burrows and borings they leave in soft sediments are a further indication of past life. Trace fossils provide important clues to fossil environments.

Fossils may be used to date rocks. Species that were short lived and distributed over a wide geographic area can be used to date a specific time interval. They are known as zone fossils.

CLASSIFICATION
Plants and animals are grouped at several levels. Each level is indicative of features shared by groups or by individual organisms. Proper names are given to each animal or plant. Each belongs to a species in which the individual members are almost identical. The specific name is prefixed by a generic title which groups together a number of closely related and similar species. Humans are known as *Homo sapiens*: we are warm blooded, give birth to live young, and have an internal skeleton. We belong to the Mammalia (Primates), Family Hominidae, and are vertebrates.

FOSSIL PLANTS
These range from single-celled organisms through to the giant redwoods, the oak, and smaller flowering plants. Although they are slightly less important than fossil animals, spores and pollen are useful in the dating of rocks, and plants are important in defining the environments that existed on land in ancient times. Mineralized wood is among the most beautiful of fossils.

Plants from the Age of Coal
Coal Measure plants represent one of the best-known and most diverse floras recorded in geological history. Delicate fronds and robust stems and roots can be found on the spoil heaps of coal mines in Wales, the Midlands, the north-east of England, and Scotland.

Lepidodendron (Lycopod)

Family: Lepidodendraceae

Age: Carboniferous.
Distribution: Worldwide.
Appearance and fossil facts: Members of the lycopod group include the living club mosses but, during the Carboniferous Period, giant trees, such as *Lepidodendron*, grew to more than 30 metres in height. *Lepidodendron* had strong, robust roots and stem. The stem branched in repeated forks. It is covered in leaf scars that spiral

around its diameter. These are oval to subtriangular in shape. The roots of *Lepidodendron* are named *Stigmaria* and the leaves *Sigillaria*.

Calamites

Family: Sphenopsidae

Age: Carboniferous
(Pennsylvanian).
Distribution: Worldwide.
Appearance and fossil facts:
Calamites is an ancient relative of
the modern horsetail, the jointed-
stemmed plants that plague
gardeners. *Calamites*, however,
was over 12 metres high. The
trunk is ridged vertically with
branches arising at the joints.
Fossils are commonly found in
sandy sediments associated with
coal seams. These sediments were
deposited in a delta environment.

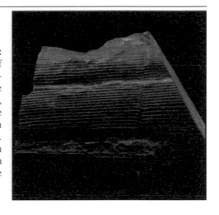

Annularia

Family: Sphenopsidae

Age: Carboniferous
(Pennsylvanian).
Distribution: Worldwide.
Appearance and fossil facts:
Coal Measure slabs adorned with
the remains of *Annularia* are
among the more treasured Coal
Measure plant fossils. The
remains occur as black,
carbonaceous traces over the rock
surface, the original tissue having
been altered after burial.
Annularia are the detached leaves
of the sphenopsid *Calamites*.
They are composed of thin
individual leaflets organized into
circlets around a thin stem.

Annularia is closely related to *Sphenophyllum* which is also found throughout the
world.

These are fern-like plants from the Carboniferous Period, but they produced seeds and not spores. The leaf fronds are very similar to those of true ferns.

Alethopteris

Family: Medullosaceae

Age: Carboniferous–Early Permian.
Distribution: Northern Hemisphere.
Appearance and fossil facts: *Alethopteris* and related forms, such as *Neuropteris* and *Pecopteris*, are often beautifully preserved on the surfaces of coaliferous sediments. *Alethopteris* has large, intricate fronds composed of medium-length, subrounded leaflets which are attached to one another at the base by tissue. Each leaflet has a simple venation, with the subsidiary veins arising almost at right-angles from the central vein. The leaflets are straighter and thinner than those of *Neuropteris*. The genus is found throughout Europe, Asia, North Africa, and North America.

By the Triassic Period, the Coal Measure floras and many of the species found in them had disappeared. Mesozoic floras were characterized by true ferns, seed ferns, cycads, conifers, and redwoods. Flowering plants became commonplace 100 million years ago.

Ginkgo

Family: Ginkgoaceae

Age: Late Triassic–Recent.
Distribution: Worldwide.
Appearance and fossil facts: We can trace the ancestry of the living Maidenhair Tree for over 200 million years. During the Mesozoic Era, large ginkgos were commonplace, with numerous species present during the Jurassic Period. Fossil ginkgos are known mostly by their leaves which were broad and fern shaped, and invariably subdivided and lobed. The leaf venation is parallel to the length of the leaf, and the leaves themselves occur in clusters. The ginkgos are among the oldest-known, non-flowering, vascular plants. *Ginkgo biloba* occurs naturally today in China and North America; ornamental trees are grown in botanical gardens and arboretums.

Araucaria

Family: Araucariaceae

Age: Jurassic–Recent.
Distribution: Worldwide.
Appearance and fossil facts: *Araucaria*, the Monkey-puzzle and Norfolk Island Pine trees, belong to the conifer group of non-flowering plants. The leaves are small and narrow, and spirally arranged around the branch. Large rounded cones are typical, with the scales having a spiral arrangement. Polished sections of cones reveal seeds set in woody tissue. Living representatives of this genus are native to the Southern Hemisphere. Fossil species lived in subtropical forests on mountainsides. Araucarids are found throughout the world, having first appeared in the Jurassic. Silicified cones are comparatively common fossils.

Williamsonia

Family: Bennettitales

Age: Late Triassic–Cretaceous.
Distribution: Worldwide.
Appearance and fossil facts: Illustrations of Mesozoic landscapes, crowded with dinosaurs, also include various species of plants with short, stumpy, or branching stems. These belong to the Bennettitales or cycadeoids, which are somewhat similar to the modern sago palms. *Wiliamsonia* grew to a height of about 3 metres, and branched irregularly; its foliage was palm-like. The bark had a diamond-shaped pattern, and the 'flower' was star shaped with a disc-like base and large, petal-like stems that curved upwards and inwards. *Williamsonia* is associated with a tropical forest environment. Sister groups, such as *Pterophyllum*, possessed fern-like leaves with parallel venation.

FLOWERING PLANTS

The flowering plants, or angiosperms, first appeared during the Jurassic Period. They are classified into single-seed and two-seed groupings – the monocotyledons and dicotyledons. The first have leaves with a straight venation; plants of the second group are characterized by a network of veins.

Laurus (Laurel)

Family: Lauraceae
Dicotyledonous Angiosperm

Age: Cretaceous–Recent.
Distribution: Worldwide.
Appearance and fossil facts: The laurel is among the most ancient of flowering plants. It first appeared during the Cretaceous, and was an important component of the subtropical/temperate forest that flourished towards the end of the Age of Dinosaurs. The leaves are elongate, with undivided edges and well-defined venation. The secondary veins are offset, branching forwards and outwards from the central vein. Like all fossil leaves, those of laurel are best preserved in very fine-grained sediments, and rapid burial is an important factor in their preservation.

Betula (Birch)

Family: Betulaceae
Dicotyledonous Angiosperm

Age: Tertiary–Recent.
Distribution: Worldwide.
Appearance and fossil facts: The living birch is dicotyledonous like its ancient ancestors. It was an important component of Miocene to Recent floras, with the forests of the Northern Hemisphere having similar characteristics to their modern counterparts. The birch leaf is broad and fan shaped, with a strongly developed venation that forks out

across the leaf from the central vein. The leaf edge is very slightly serrated. Excellent specimens of birch and other angiosperms can be found in leaf-beds scattered throughout Europe. These occur in areas that were once covered by ponds and lakes; the leaves of the plants were rapidly buried by a fine drape of mud in conditions that lacked oxygen. *Betula* was commonplace in Ice Age forests, with individual trees exceeding 15 metres in height.

Nipa (Nipadites)

Family: Arecaceae
(Monocotyledonous Angiosperm)

Age: Cretaceous–Recent.
Distribution: Northern Hemisphere.
Appearance and fossil facts: *Nipa* is a stemless palm that, today, is found near mangrove swamps and river banks in tropical south-east Asia. It grows to 1.5 metres, and has long, frond-like leaves that grow upwards and outwards from a pointed stump. The fronds are divided into leaflets which are slightly offset along the branch. Coconut-like seeds of *Nipa* are found in the Tertiary age sands and clays of Belgium and the Isle of Sheppey in south-eastern England. In today's *Nipa* palms, the seeds grow near the base of the frond. Several seeds occur in a fibrous husk. Fossil seeds range in length from about 15 to 40 centimetres.

Stromatolite

Order: Cyanophyta
(Blue-green Algae)

Age: Precambrian–Recent.
Distribution: Worldwide.
Appearance and fossil facts: Stromatolites are layered structures composed of calcium carbonate. The structure is formed in shallow, tropical, tidal to subtidal environments when fine detrital material adheres to the glutinous surfaces of blue-green algae. These are among the simplest of plants. They are single celled, and often occur as filaments. The robust, laminated stromatolites are wave resistant, and beautiful examples survive today in Sharks Bay, South Australia. Stromatolites, such as *Collenia*, were among the first forms of life on Earth, their history dating back 3.5 billion years. Other groups of algae secrete calcareous frameworks. Their remains have been important rock-builders over the last 600 million years.

Fossil Wood

Age: Permian–Recent.
Distribution: Worldwide.
Appearance and fossil facts: The petrified forests of North America provide us with an insight into the great forests that existed, particularly during the Triassic Period. Huge tree-trunks, 30 metres or more long, are commonplace, and the appearance of their internal structure is enhanced by the presence of chalcedonic and opaline silica. Silicified wood is the product of silica replacement; the silica enters and replaces the original woody tissues from fluids that passed through the sediment in which the tree was buried. Impurities in the silica may give rise to vibrant colours. Fossil wood is found throughout the world. The petrified forests of North America were composed mainly of conifers. The fossil tree trunks of Lulworth (Dorset) and the fossil forest in Glasgow (Scotland) are famous examples in the United Kingdom.

FORAMINIFERA

Many single-celled animals deposit a skeleton, or test. This is usually composed of calcium carbonate, but some use chitin and some stick grains of sand and other materials together to form a rigid structure. Sea-floor-dwelling foraminiferids are termed benthonic whereas species that float in the upper waters of the oceans are referred to as planktonic. Various species occur as rock-builders throughout the world. Many are used to date rocks. Foraminiferal tests first appear in Cambrian deposits.

Nummulites

Family: Nummulitidae

Age: Palaeocene–Oligocene.

Distribution: Countries bordering the Mediterranean and Caribbean Seas (Tethys).

Appearance and fossil facts: Some species of nummulite grew to 11 centimetres in diameter. More commonly, individuals range from 5 millimetres to 2 centimentres in size. The test is round or discoidal, flat or slightly inflated. The outer surface is marked with a curved or spiral ornamentation, and some species have a rather rough, 'sand-grain' appearance owing to the presence of pillars. Nummulites are found as rock-formers in many areas of Europe, Africa, and Asia, and are important in helping to determine the age of rocks and the environment that prevailed in the area at that time. Examples of nummulite tests can be collected from the foreshore in Alum Bay on the Isle of Wight, southern England.

Globigerina

Family: Globigerinidae

Age: Palaeozoic–Recent.
Distribution: Worldwide.
Appearance and fossil facts:
Planktonic foraminiferids first
appeared during the Jurassic Period.
They were adapted to a floating
mode of life, and their fossils are
found in sediments that usually
indicate deep-water environments.

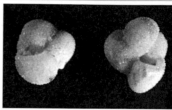

Various genera and species are included under the umbrella term
'globigerinid'; they are globular, rough-textured forms which indicate life at
different levels in the water column, or even different temperatures. Many
species are short lived and distributed over a wide geographical area. They are
extremely useful in the correlation of rocks worldwide.

Textularia

Family: Textulariidae

Age: Cretaceous–Recent.
Distribution: Worldwide.
Appearance and fossil facts: Textulariids have tests composed of sand-sized
grains. These are stuck together by the animal to form a rigid external skeleton.
The grains are usually limestone or quartz fragments. Specific forms are
diagnostic of shallow, inshore environments or the deeper waters of the abyssal
plain. The type of grain and the overall architecture of the specimen help to
determine the water depth in which the animals lived. Overall, the agglutinates,
as these animals are called, are less important in the dating and correlation of
rocks throughout the world.

SPONGES

Living sponges inhabit mainly marine environments throughout the world although the larger forms are confined largely to tropical and subtropical waters. Sponges are simple, multi-celled invertebrate animals which have an internal skeleton composed of loose or fused spicules. The spicules vary in size and shape, and may be calcareous, siliceous, or horny in their composition.

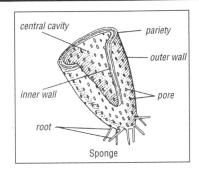

Raphidonema

Family: Lelapiidae

Age: Mesozoic.
Distribution: Europe.
Appearance and fossil facts:

Raphidonema is a robust, calcareous sponge best known from the Farringdon Sponge Gravels of southern England. The skeleton is thick walled, sturdy, and cup shaped or irregularly formed. Individuals range in size from 1.6 to 4.7 centimetres. The spicules are three rayed. The outer

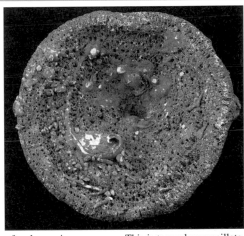

surface of this sponge is often lumpy in appearance. This is termed mammillate, and, together with a rough surface texture and brown coloration from iron staining, make *Raphidonema* a good specimen for your personal collection. In life, water passed through the large pores that are found on the surface of the skeleton.

Ventriculites (Rhizopterion)

Family: Ventriculitidae

Age: Cretaceous.
Distribution: Europe–Asia.
Appearance and fossil facts: *Ventriculites* is a representative of the group known as the glass sponges. It is shaped like a vase or funnel, and individuals may reach 10 centimetres in height. These animals may be locally common or even abundant in the Late Cretaceous Chalk rocks of Europe. The skeleton is composed of six-rayed spicules which are fused together to form a rectangular mesh. The spicules are siliceous, and this helps in the preservation of the delicate skeletal structure. There are small, root-like structures present at the base of the skeleton. The correct name for *Ventriculites infundibuliformis* is *Rhizopterion*.

Cliona

Family: Clionidae

Age: Devonian–Recent.
Distribution: Worldwide.
Appearance and fossil facts: This unique sponge is known mostly from the traces it leaves on other fossils. *Cliona* is a boring, or burrowing, sponge which actually tunnels into shells or rock surfaces. Typically, the fossil is recognized by the presence of small, node-like structures which are interconnected by thin tubes or rods. *Cliona* is commonly found on or in chert or flint nodules from the Late Cretaceous chalks of England and northern France.

CORALS

Corals are multicelled animals with a well-defined body cavity known as a coelom. They belong to the Coelenterata. The body is polypoid, with tentacles around a centrally placed mouth. Corals deposit calcareous skeletons which may be single or colonial in form.

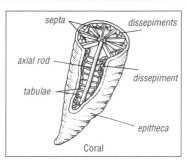

Coral

TABULATE CORALS

Colonial corals were represented by numerous genera during the Palaeozoic Era. Skeletons were made up of many small corallites with few internal structures. They are found in sediments ranging from Ordovician to Permian in age.

Favosites

Family: Favositidae

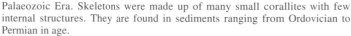

Age: Ordovician–Devonian.
Distribution: Worldwide.
Appearance and fossil facts: The individual corallites of *Favosites* are pentagonal (five sided). They have short spinose septa inside the cup, separated by small horizontal plates called tabulae. These are closely spaced and robust in character. Interconnecting pores occur between corallites. The complete skeleton, or corallum, is irregularly shaped but may grow into flattened or slightly rounded heads 30 to 45 centimetres across. *Favosites* is particularly abundant in the muddy limestones of the Welsh Borderlands. It lived in shallow, tropical marine environments.

Syringopora

Family: Syringoporidae

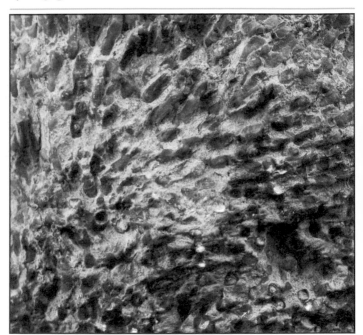

Age: Silurian–Late Carboniferous.
Distribution: Worldwide.
Appearance and fossil facts: *Syringopora* formed large colonies. The skeleton is composed of thin, cylindrical corallites that are connected by numerous horizontal processes. The septa are small, and spinose or sometimes ridge-like, but are usually difficult to see with the naked eye. The tabulae are well developed, and relatively thin but numerous. The presence of twelve spinose septa is diagnostic of some species. *Syringopora* is commonly found in Silurian and Carboniferous limestones. Numerous specimens have been retrieved from quarries in the Welsh Borderlands and from along the coastlines of England and Wales.

RUGOSE CORALS

Rugose corals may be single or colonial in form. They are commonly known as the 'stony' corals, and have well-developed septa, dissepiments, and tabulae. They range in time from the Ordovician to the Permian.

Siphonodendron (Lithostrotion)   Family: Lithostrotionidae

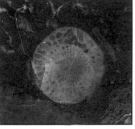

Age: Carboniferous.
Distribution: Worldwide.
Appearance and fossil facts: *Siphonodendron* is better known as *Lithostrotion*, and the species '*Lithostrotion*' *junceum* is one of the most familiar of all British fossils. It is found in Carboniferous limestones throughout the British Isles. *Lithostrotion* formed massive colonies with rounded to hexagonally shaped corallites – the latter being found in the species *L. basaltiformis*. The corallites are usually tightly packed or touching. Internally there was a small central rod or boss surrounded by well-developed septa; the septa are relatively short and thickened. The tabulae are conical. Some skeletons have been impregnated by silica and, when etched in very dilute acid, the more insoluble corallites stand proud from the enclosing sediment. Etched colonies have a life-like appearance.

Caninia   Family: Caninidae

Age: Carboniferous–Permian.
Distribution: Europe, North America, Asia.
Appearance and fossil facts: *Caninia* is a large, single (solitary) coral. It may be cone shaped but the vast majority of specimens are cylindrical and gently curved. As with other rugose corals, the external surface of *Caninia* is rough textured. Growth lines circle the corallite, which may thicken and thin where regeneration has taken place. The septa are short and dilated with numerous dissepiments evident inside the outer wall. Many thin, flat tabulae can be seen in a polished section of the coral. *Caninia* may grow up to 30 to 45 centimetres in length. These corals are found most commonly in muddy Carboniferous limestones.

HEXACORALS OR SCLERACTINIANS
Living corals are included in this group. They may be solitary or colonial, and have prominent septa and dissepiments. They first appeared during the Triassic Period.

Thamnasteria

Family: Thamnasteridae

Age: Triassic–Cretaceous.
Distribution: Europe, North America, South America, Asia.
Appearance and fossil facts: This is a medium to massive coral with branched or encrusting forms. Individual corallites are small to medium in size; they lack well-defined walls. The septa tend to merge or fuse at the edges of the corallites. They extend inwards to the centre of the corallite where a thin axial structure can be seen. *Thamnasteria* is frequently found in association with another scleractinian, *Isastrea*, in the Jurassic limestones of southern England. These corals were important reef builders during the Jurassic Period. The best specimens can be found in muddy limestones or clays. *Isastrea* is more robust with five- or six-sided corallites separated by thin, ridge-like outer walls.

Turbinolia

Family: Turbinolidae

Age: Eocene–Recent.
Distribution: Worldwide.
Appearance and fossil facts: *Turbinolia* is a small, solitary hexacoral with a horn-shaped skeleton. The major septa are well developed and they give the outside of the corallite a ridged appearance. The central columella is star shaped. Septal ridges extend over the upper surface of the outer wall. *Turbinolia*, and other small solitary corals, are commonly found in Tertiary limestones and deeper-water claystones. They can live in several thousand metres of water. This would imply that some species existed in the aphotic zone where the water is so deep that light never penetrates it.

BRYOZOANS

Bryozoans are colonial organisms that secrete calcareous skeletons. They can be delicate or massive. Some forms are plant-like while others are very similar to corals in their appearance.

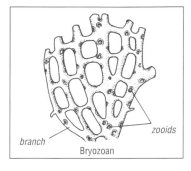

branch   zooids
Bryozoan

Fenestella

Family: Fenestellidae

Age: Ordovician–Permian.
Distribution: Europe, North America.
Appearance and fossil facts: Commonly known as the 'lace' bryozoan, *Fenestella* is frequently found in sediments of Carboniferous age. The skeleton is usually large with many slender branches radiating outwards to form a funnel-shaped colony. The branches are linked by

horizontal crossbars, or dissepiments, which are thinner and probably hollow. Small openings pock the surfaces of branches. These lead into tiny living chambers or zooecia. The bryozoans are possibly related to the brachiopods. They were essentially filter feeders, drawing food into the colony by the gentle movement of myriads of microscopic organisms.

Archimedes

Family: Archimedidae

Age: Carboniferous–Permian.
Distribution: Europe, North Africa, Asia.
Appearance and fossil facts: One of the most easily recognized bryozoans, *Archimedes* is formed around a screw-like axis. The axis is solid but it supports a delicately structured frond. This is spiralled and lace-like, with each branch exhibiting two rows of openings. The spiral growth is achieved by the

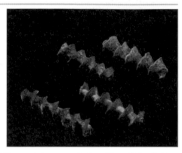

localized deposition of skeletal tissue. The openings mark the sites of the living chambers or zooecia. The actual frond is rarely preserved, although exceptional fossils can be found in Carboniferous muddy limestones. The central axis is often fragmented but some specimens reach 15 centimetres in height. *Archimedes* lived in relatively quiet, tropical to subtropical environments.

Berenicea

Family: Berenicidae

Age: Ordovician–Recent.
Distribution: Worldwide.
Appearance and fossil facts: Only specialist collectors look for fossils such as *Berenicea*. A close look, however, at a fossil echinoid or bivalve found in the Chalk rocks of northern Europe may reveal the presence of this attractive, encrusting bryozoan. *Berenicea* itself is almost microscopic in size but colonies of 2 to 3 centimetres across may be

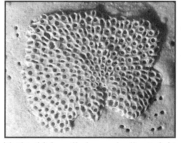

found. The colony is almost circular, with the thick-walled zooecia directed, in terms of growth, outwards and slightly upwards. They have rounded apertures. The colony radiates outwards from a central core area. This genus is most frequently found in Jurassic and Cretaceous limestones.

BRACHIOPODS

The brachiopods are an ancient group of invertebrates that first appeared during the Cambrian Period. There are a few living representatives of the group but brachiopods are essentially linked with the Palaeozoic Era. Exclusively marine animals, they were characterized by a two-valved shell in which the valves were of unequal size. The group, or phylum, is divided into two classes, commonly known as the inarticulates and the articulates.

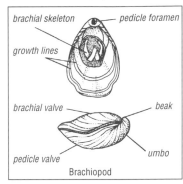

Brachiopod

brachial skeleton — pedicle foramen
growth lines
brachial valve — beak
pedicle valve — umbo

INARTICULATES

These relatively primitive brachiopods have small, rounded to elongate shells, with a poorly defined hinge line, no teeth, and no sockets. There are no internal structures to support the feeding organ, and the shell is often made of a horny organic (chitinophosphate) material although calcareous external skeletons (exoskeletons) are known in various genera.

Lingula

Family: Lingulidae

Age: Cambrian–Recent.
Distribution: Worldwide.
Appearance and fossil facts: *Lingula* is a survivor! The first species appeared during the Cambrian Period, and the genus still survives today in intertidal environments of Asia. Adapted to a burrowing mode of life, the animal has an elongate, thin shell composed of two gently convex valves. These are chitinophosphatic, and are marked with fine growth lines.

Modern shells have a yellow-black, lustrous appearance. The hinge line is short and curved, and without teeth. Strongly developed muscle scars occur inside both valves. A long fleshy stalk (pedicle) occurs in living species. This is used to fix the animal inside its burrow. The pedicle is rarely found in fossils but a distinct notch is present below the beak on the pedicle valve. *Lingula* ranges in size but typical specimens attain a length of 2 centimetres.

ARTICULATES
These have a well-developed hinge line, and the shells are invariably calcareous. Internal support structures are also present in many families.

Dalmanella

Family: Dalmanellidae

Age: Ordovician–Silurian.
Distribution: Worldwide.
Appearance and fossil facts: *Dalmanella* is a small- to medium-sized articulate brachiopod. It is an orthid, having two convex valves with a ribbed ornamentation. Orthids are strophic brachiopods in which the width of the hinge line is equal to, or greater than, the width of the shell. In *Dalmanella*, the two are equal, with the hinge sloping gently away from the pedicle area. The pedicle opening is triangular in shape. *Dalmanella* is well known from the Ordovician to Silurian sediments of Wales and the Welsh Borderlands. Individual specimens measure 2 centimetres across.

Orthis

Family: Orthidae

Age: Cambrian–Ordovician.
Distribution: Worldwide.
Appearance and fossil facts: *Orthis* is a small- to medium-sized brachiopod. Unlike that of *Dalmanella*, the brachial, or smaller, valve is not essentially convex. It is generally flattened, exhibiting a long, straight hinge line. In the pedicle valve, the pedicle notch is triangular, and a large interarea is present. *Orthis* is strongly ribbed, with the ribs radiating outwards from the centre of the hinge line. Orthids were an important component of Ordovician faunas, and various species can be found in Wales, the Lake District, and Scotland. Specimens range in size from 1 to 3 centimetres.

Leptaena

Family: Leptaenidae

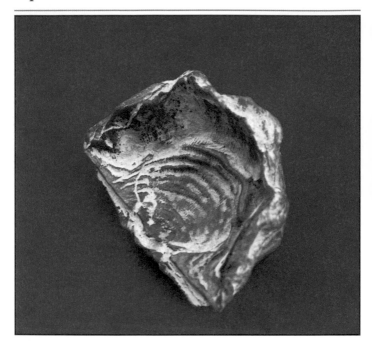

Age: Middle Ordovician–Devonian.
Distribution: Worldwide.
Appearance and fossil facts: This medium-sized brachiopod has a semicircular shape. The brachial valve is concave and the pedicle valve convex. In section, the shell bends anteriorly to give an L-shaped profile. The external surface is covered with fine radial striations and strongly developed, concentric growth ridges, or *rugae*. *Leptaena* rested on the sea-floor with the brachial valve buried in the sediment. The shape of the shell prevented sediment from entering into the body cavity during the feeding process. *Leptaena* is commonly found in Silurian rocks of the Welsh Borderlands. Typical specimens measure 4 centimetres across.

Chonetes

Family: Chonetidae

Age: Devonian–Permian.
Distribution: Worldwide.
Appearance and fossil facts: *Chonetes* is characterized by a semicircular shell, a long hinge line, and a pitted, finely ribbed ornament. It is a small, articulate brachiopod in which the pedicle valve is convex and the brachial valve flattened. Ear-like extensions (auricles) developed at the edges of the hinge line. Internally, well-developed muscle scars occur, and a median plate (septum) is present in each valve. *Chonetes* is noted for the presence of a row of spines along the edge of the pedicle valve. These spines are thought to have supported the shell in a soft substrate. *Chonetes* measured 2 centimetres across the hinge line.

Productus

Family: Productidae

Age: Carboniferous.
Distribution: Europe and Asia.
Appearance and fossil facts: Large to very large specimens of productid brachiopods are found in the Carboniferous limestones of the British Isles. *Productus* is a medium-sized genus, but the shells of *Gigantoproductus* may reach a width of 15 centimetres. *Productus* has a hemispherical shape, in which the pedicle valve is markedly convex and the brachial valve flat or slightly concave. The latter is almost circular and is essentially lid-like. The valves are covered with rugae, faint ribs, pustules, and many are spinose. The majority of fossils recovered from limestones are 3 to 4 centimetres in size.

Conchidium

Family: Pentameridae

Age: Silurian–Devonian.
Distribution: Worldwide.
Appearance and fossil facts:
Superficially, *Conchidium* resembles
a productid brachiopod. It is,
however, a pentamerid with a
strongly biconvex shell and a short
hinge line. It also has a very strong
beak on the pedicle valve which
curves over to overlap the
corresponding feature on the brachial
valve. Both valves have a strongly

ribbed ornament with poorly defined growth lines. This robust brachiopod is
found in limestones throughout the world. Individual specimens reach 4
centimetres in size.

Sellithyris

Family: Sellithyridae

Age: Cretaceous.
Distribution: Europe.
**Appearance and fossil
facts:** *Sellithyris* is a
small- to medium-sized
brachiopod. The shell is
biconvex although a
variety of shapes may
occur in a population
that includes juveniles
and mature specimens.
The shell is smooth
with well-developed
concentric growth

lines. Two closely spaced folds occur on the anterior area. The pedicle foramen
is very well defined, circular in outline, and occurs at the tip of the umbo. The
hinge line is curved. Internally, a well-developed brachial skeleton supported
the feeding organs. Large specimens of *Sellithyris* reach 2.5 centimetres in
length. Numerous examples may be found along the southern coastline of the
Isle of Wight.

Goniorhynchia

Family: Rhynchonellidae

Age: Jurassic.
Distribution: Europe.
Appearance and fossil facts: This is a medium-sized brachiopod with a biconvex shell. A prominent beak is present on the pedicle valve. Both valves are strongly folded anteriorly, with a well-defined sulcus present on the brachial valve. The line of opening between the two valves interlocks because of the folded and serrated nature of the valve margins. Prominent radial ribs ornament both valves. The denticulate aperture enables the organism to filter out grains of sand from the currents entering the body chamber. *Goniorhynchia* is commonly found in the Jurassic sediments of England. It grew to 2 centimetres in length.

MOLLUSCS

The molluscs are a large and diverse group of invertebrates. They range in time from the Cambrian to Recent, and include gastropods, bivalves, and cephalopods (e.g. squids, cuttlefish, ammonites).

GASTROPODS

Gastropods have a single-valved shell which may be coiled in a flat plane or in a helical spiral. The shell develops around a central columella, and may consist of several whorls or complete coils. Coiling, ornament, and the shape of the aperture are among the characteristics used in the identification of given species. Gastropods first appear in the Cambrian Period.

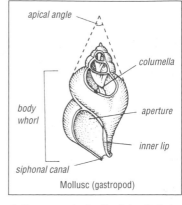

Mollusc (gastropod)

Bellerophon

Family: Bellerophontidae

Age: Silurian–Triassic.
Distribution: Worldwide.
Appearance and fossil facts: The shell of *Bellerophon* is coiled in a single plane, and exhibits a bilateral symmetry – each half of the shell being identical. The shell broadens markedly towards the aperture, with the last whorl covering the earlier ones. The aperture is marked by the

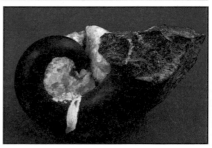

presence of a deep slit which is 'healed' as growth continues. This results in the development of a strong ridge that continues backwards around the midline of each whorl. The outer whorl may be ribbed and slightly nodular in appearance. *Bellerophon* shells grew to a width of 8 centimetres.

Natica

Family: Naticidae

Age: Palaeocene–Recent.
Distribution: Worldwide.
Appearance and fossil facts: Commonly known as the 'moon' shell, *Natica* is a medium-sized gastropod characterized by a conical to spherical shape. The spire is low and the whorls have steep walls. The aperture is large, and oval to circular in shape with a thickened inner lip. The shell is smooth or discretely ribbed owing to growth lines. Naticids are carnivorous, drilling circular holes into the shells of their prey. Excellent specimens of *Natica* are commonly found in the marine Tertiary of southern England. An adult shell will reach 5 centimetres high.

Aporrhais

Family: Aporrhaidae

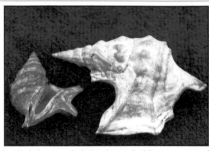

Age: Jurassic–Recent.
Distribution: Worldwide.
Appearance and fossil facts:
Aporrhais is frequently found in clay-rich sediments of Cretaceous to Tertiary age. Complete specimens can be quite spectacular, with large- to medium-sized shells characterized by a very large, flared, notched, and spinose outer lip. The shell terminates at a narrow angle. Each whorl is slightly rounded, having a bold ornament of growth lines, vertical ridges, and tubercules. *Aporrhais* rested on the sea-floor or created a shallow burrow. Large specimens can reach 12 centimetres in height.

Conus

Family: Conidae

Age: Cretaceous–Recent.
Distribution: Worldwide.
Appearance and fossil facts: *Conus* is a small to large gastropod. The shell is shaped like an upturned cone with a flat or low conical spire. The walls of the outer whorl are steep, and the aperture is long and narrow with parallel sides. A distinct notch occurs on the upper end of the aperture; this leads into a small canal. The outer lip is thin. Spiral grooves and ridges form the ornament. *Conus* lives in fairly shallow marine environments, and fossils are most commonly found in sandy clays and calcareous sandstones. It is best known from the Tertiary beds of the London and Hampshire basins, and the Paris basin in France.

Archimediella (Turritella)

Family: Turritellidae

Age: Eocene–Recent.
Distribution: Worldwide.
Appearance and fossil facts: *Archimediella* has a long, tapering shell which terminates in an acute angle and turreted spire. Specimens reach a length of 6 to 8 centimetres. The spire is composed of numerous whorls which slightly overhang each other to give a shouldered appearance. Each whorl usually has a spiral-ridged ornament although smooth forms, lacking ornament, have been recorded. The aperture is entire. *Archimediella* is a shallow burrower; hundreds of specimens live in small areas of sea-floor. It is a common fossil of the Eocene rocks of southern England and the Paris Basin.

SCAPHOPODS

Scaphopods, or 'tooth shells', are known from Late Cambrian times. They have long, cylindrical shells.

Dentalium

Family: Dentaliidae

Age: Middle Triassic –Recent.
Distribution: Worldwide.
Appearance and fossil facts: *Dentalium* has a typically cylindrical shell. It is long and gently curved, having a tusk-like appearance. In life, the foot and tentacles of the head appear from the larger aperture; and waste materials are expelled from the smaller opening at the tapered end. Scaphopods can be smooth, but several genera, including *Dentalium*, have vertically ridged ornaments. *Dentalium* is common in the Eocene, and shells range from 1 to 8 centimetres in length.

CEPHALOPODS

Living representatives of this group include the squids, octopuses, and cuttlefishes. These cephalopods have tentacled heads and internal shells. The living *Nautilus* has, in contrast, an external skeleton that encloses the soft parts of the body. The soft parts of the body are essentially confined to the outer (last) chamber although a tube (siphuncle) extends back through all the preceding chambers. This contains soft tissue associated with gasses released into the chambers to give buoyancy. The ventral or peripheral, side of the shell, or the circumference, is termed the venter.

NAUTILOIDS

Nautiloids first appeared during the Cambrian Period. They were major representatives of Palaeozoic communities, with straight- and coiled-shell varieties occupying different niches in marine environments.

Orthoceras

Family: Orthoceratidae

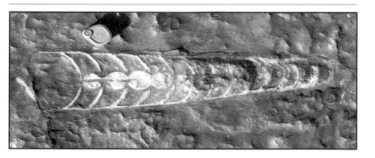

Age: Middle Ordovician.
Distribution: Europe, North America.
Appearance and fossil facts: *Orthoceras* has a long, tapering, cylindrical shell which is divided into chambers. The septa, or walls, between the chambers are simple, and there is a hole for the siphuncle, found in the centre. In life, the siphuncle, or tube, extends backwards from the body into the chambers of the shell. The external surface of the shell is either smooth or slightly furrowed. Individual shells grew to 20 centimetres in length. *Orthoceras* was a free-swimming animal which normally moved roughly horizontally but which sometimes also 'hovered' at an angle to the sea-floor in its search for food.

Nautilus

Family: Nautilidae

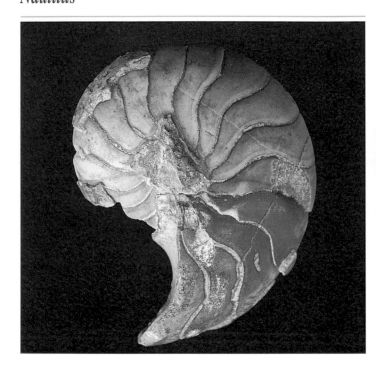

Age: Triassic–Recent.
Distribution: Worldwide.
Appearance and fossil facts: *Nautilus* has a medium to large shell in which the outer chambers enclose the earlier inner chambers. This type of shell is termed involute. The septa, or walls, between the chambers are simple, and the siphuncle is found in the lower central area of this partition. The external surface of the shell is usually smooth, but slightly furrowed species existed during the Eocene epoch. Individual shells grew to 40 centimetres in diameter. *Nautilus* was a free-swimming animal that, today, lives in the open sea. Changes in shell buoyancy enable the animal to rise and descend vertically through the water in search of food.

AMMONOIDS

In palaeontological terms, ammonoids are the most important group of molluscs. They first evolved during the Devonian Period, and were an important component of Palaeozoic and of Mesozoic communities. An ammonoid has an external shell that is divided into chambers. A well-defined suture line is often visible on the external surface of the test. It marks the contact between the outer wall and the internal partitions between chambers. The form of the suture and the position of the siphuncle are very important in the recognition of the various types of ammonoids.

Goniatites

Family: Goniatitidae

Age: Early Carboniferous.
Distribution: Worldwide.
Appearance and fossil facts: The shell of *Goniatites* is small to medium sized, with individual specimens rarely exceeding 6 centimetres in diameter. It is globular, with the outer whorls overlapping earlier or preceding structures. The term used to describe this is 'involute'. *Goniatites* has a small initial area of coiling (umbilicus), with the whorls gradually broadening towards the aperture. The suture line is divided into angular lobes. Normally, these are covered by a small external layer. *Goniatites* is often abundant in the Lower Carboniferous sediments of South Wales and England.

Gastrioceras

Family: Gastrioceratidae

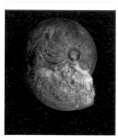

Age: Carboniferous.
Distribution: Worldwide.
Appearance and fossil facts: Although it is a member of the same superfamily as *Goniatites*, *Gastrioceras* is characterized by a broad, deep umbilicus and flatter shell. The whorls only partly overlap, and the test is therefore less involute than in *Goniatites*. Small tubercules and ribs may occur as an external ornament on the flanks and upper surface of the shell. The suture is folded into lobes and saddles which are more rounded towards the anterior. *Gastrioceras* is frequently found in marine bands associated with the coal deposits of the Late Carboniferous. It has a diameter of approximately 7 centimetres.

Ceratites

Family: Ceratitidae

Age: Middle Triassic.

Distribution: Europe.

Appearance and fossil facts: The shell of *Ceratites* is discoidal with a broad umbilical area. It is essentially 'open-coiled' (evolute) with only a slight overhang of the interior whorls. The whorls increase in height towards the aperture. They

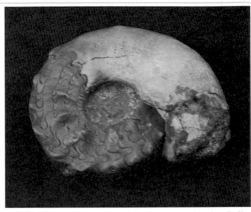

are almost box-like in section. Strong ribs, nodes, and tubercules give the shell a rather coarse ornament. The suture lines are closely spaced, each divided into rounded lobes and saddles which may be subdivided or tooth-like in outline. Lobes are directed forwards while saddles face to the rear. *Ceratites* is an important fossil from the Middle Triassic of Europe. Related forms are also recorded in North America. Individual specimens may reach up to 10 centimetres in diameter.

AMMONITES

Ammonites are characterized by a complex suture line. They have a diversity of forms and are used as zone fossils for Mesozoic sediments throughout the world.

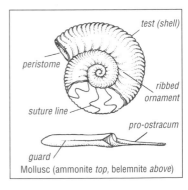

test (shell)

peristome

ribbed ornament

suture line

pro-ostracum

guard

Mollusc (ammonite *top*, belemnite *above*)

Phylloceras

Family: Phylloceratidae

Age: Early Jurassic–Early Cretaceous.
Distribution: Worldwide.
Appearance and fossil facts:
Phylloceras is a small- to medium-sized ammonite with an involute shell and a complex suture line. The shell is compressed, with rather flattened sides, and the umbilicus is small. The suture line is often described as frilly, with both lobes and saddles subdivided with minor frills. The external surface is usually smooth but a simple ornament of fine 'growth' lines is known in some species. Typically, *Phylloceras* reaches 10 to 15 centimetres in diameter.

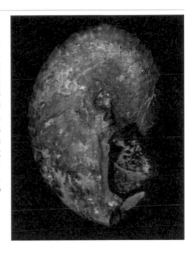

Dactylioceras

Family: Dactylioceratidae

Age: Early Jurassic.
Distribution: Worldwide.
Appearance and fossil facts:
Dactylioceras is a medium-sized ammonite. It is particularly well known from the Early Jurassic sediments of the Yorkshire coast of England. The test is coiled like a rope (evolute), with little or no overlap between adjacent whorls. The umbilicus is wide and shallow. Each whorl is marked by a strong ribbing, with the ribs forked on the ventral surface. The ribs are slightly flattened on the venter.
Individual shells reach 8 centimetres in diameter. Museum specimens sometimes have a serpent's head carved on the anterior chambers. These 'petrified serpents' were sold to pilgrims in medieval times.

Perisphinctes

Family: Perisphinctidae

Age: Late Jurassic.

Distribution: Europe, Africa, Asia, Caribbean.

Appearance and fossil facts: Perisphinctid ammonites can be very large, with 30-centimetre specimens commonplace. *Perisphinctes* has an evolute test with a slight overlap of preceding whorls. The whorls are deep with a box-like section. The umbilicus is quite wide with steep shoulders to the initial whorls. Closely spaced ribs occur on the walls of the inner whorls. These become more strongly defined and more widely spaced in the last whorl. The ventral surface is smooth over its anterior area. The suture is usually poorly defined on the external surface. *Perisphinctes* probably lived in deeper waters; its centres of buoyancy and gravity are relatively far apart. Experimentation has inferred that this is typical of a 'slow'-moving ammonite that took time to change its position in terms of direction and water depth.

Douvilliceras

Family: Douvilliceratidae

Age: Early Cretaceous.
Distribution: Worldwide.
Appearance and fossil facts: *Douvilliceras* has a strongly ribbed shell. The ribs stand proud of the shell surface, passing across the rounded venter. Each rib is marked with numerous tubercules or swellings. The shell is essentially evolute but there is a considerable overlap between specific whorls. The outer whorl has a rounded cross-section. Some species are spinose. *Douvilliceras* probably swam over the surface of the sea-floor searching for food. It is an important fossil in the Early Cretaceous (Albian) clay-rich sediments of Europe, North America, and Asia. Individuals grew to 10 centimetres in diameter.

Hoplites

Family: Hoplitidae

Age: Early Cretaceous.
Distribution: Europe, Asia.
Appearance and fossil facts:
Hoplitid ammonites are very important in the zonation and correlation of Lower Cretaceous sediments. *Hoplites* is a small- to medium-sized genus with an evolute shell or test. It has a relatively deep, narrow umbilicus, and the shell is laterally compressed. This results in a trapezoidal cross-section. The shell has a strongly ribbed ornament, with

the ribs branching out from a large, internal node. They may zig-zag but they do not cross over the venter. The rib endings alternate with each other. *Hoplites dentatus* is the zone fossil for the Early Middle Albian. Individual specimens may measure 5 to 10 centimetres in diameter.

Turrilites

Family: Turrilitidae

Age: Cretaceous
Distribution: Europe, Africa, North America, Asia.
Appearance and fossil facts:
Superficially *Turrilites* resembles a large, high-spired gastropod. It is, however, an aberrant ammonite which has adapted to a sedentary life on the sea-floor. Another term used to describe this genus is 'heteromorphic' (different shape). The whorls are coiled in a tight helical manner, with the end terminating in an acute apical angle. The whorls bear strong vertical ribs and tubercules. Specimens of 15 to 20 centimetres can be found in the chalks of northern Europe.

BIVALVES

Oysters, cockles, and mussels are typical bivalves. They are molluscs with shells that comprise two valves which are articulated along a hinge line and, in life, joined together by a strong, 'fibrous' ligament. Teeth and sockets can be found along the hinge line, and the animal uses two large, internal muscles to open and close the valves. The forms of the hinge line, teeth and sockets, and the muscle scars are important features

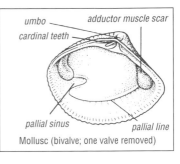

Mollusc (bivalve; one valve removed)

in the classification of the bivalves. The group first appeared during the Ordovician Period.

Venericardia (Venericor)

Family: Carditidae

Age: Palaeocene–Eocene.
Distribution: Europe, Africa, North America.
Appearance and fossil facts: *Venericardia* is a medium- to large-sized clam or bivalve. The valves are of equal size, and the shell exhibits a strong bilateral symmetry. Each valve has a trigonal shape with strong radiating ribs and well-defined radiating growth lines on the external surfaces. The hinge line is noted for the presence of three very large teeth. Internally, there are large unequally sized muscle scars connected by a complete pallial line – a strongly defined impression that marks the area occupied by the soft tissues inside the shell. The shell grew to 10 centimetres in length.

Myophorella (Trigonia)

Family: Trigoniidae

Age: Middle Triassic–Cretaceous.
Distribution: Worldwide.
Appearance and fossil facts: *Myophorella* (*Trigonia*) is well known from the Jurassic sediments of the Dorset coast. It has a triangular-shaped shell in which the valves are thick and equal in size. The valves are characterized by an ornament of concentric ridges or nodose radial ribs. A strong beak points upwards and slightly backwards, and internally two prominent teeth, each with grooves, occur on the hinge of the right valve. Individual shells can reach 8 centimetres in size.

Glycimeris

Family: Glycimeridae

Age: Cretaceous–Recent.
Distribution: Worldwide.
Appearance and fossil facts: *Glycimeris* is a small- to medium-sized bivalve with the rounded hinge line noted for the presence of numerous small teeth. The shell has an almost circular outline with an external ornament of discrete radial ribs and concentric growth lines. A well-developed beak occurs centrally, with the ligament area defined by a chevron-like pattern. Internally the two muscle scars are well developed, and the pallial line is entire. *Glycimeris* is known to burrow into shallow-water sands and sandy clays. It occurs in vast numbers in the Pliocene sediments of East Anglia and Essex. Up to 5 centimetres in size.

Carbonicola

Family: Anthracosiidae

Age: Late Carboniferous.
Distribution: Europe.
Appearance and fossil facts: *Carbonicola* is a freshwater clam from the coal swamps of the Late Carboniferous. It is small to medium in size, and has a flattened or laterally compressed shape. The hinge line is long with one or two teeth present on each valve. The beak is well developed, pointing upwards or slightly forwards. The overall shape is subtriangular, and the external ornament is limited to the presence of growth lines. Internally the anterior muscle scar is deep and circular in outline whereas the posterior scar is shallow. *Carbonicola* rarely exceeds 5 centimetres in length.

Inoceramus

Family: Inoceramidae

Age: Jurassic–Cretaceous.
Distribution: Worldwide.
Appearance and fossil facts:
Medium- to very large-sized shells of
Inoceramus are commonplace in the
Late Cretaceous chalk sediments of
Europe and North Africa. The shells
are often thin, and prisms of broken
shell debris are a common component
of Cretaceous sediments. The back
wing of the shell is more robust and
more likely to survive the rigours of

preservation. Numerous ligament pits occur on the hinge line. No teeth are present.
Externally the valves have a strongly developed ornament of large, ripple-like,
concentric ridges. The shell may be rounded or elongate in shape, flattened or
strongly convex. Individual inoceramids range between 8 and 30 centimetres in
size.

Chlamys

Family: Pectinidae

Age: Triassic–Recent.
Distribution: Worldwide.
Appearance and fossil facts:
Chlamys is a small- to medium-sized
bivalve with an inequivalve shell.
The left valve is slightly more convex
than its counterpart, but each bears an
ornament of strongly developed, box-
shaped ribs. Well-developed posterior
and anterior wings occur on either
side of the beak. *Chlamys* is a free
swimmer, and is frequently found in
calcareous sandstones and

limestones. Excellent examples occur in the Tertiary sediments of southern
England and in the Pliocene gravels of East Anglia and Essex. *Chlamys* ranges
in size from 2 to 15 centimetres.

Gervillella

Family: Gervillellidae

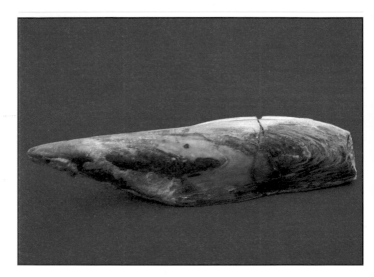

Age: Triassic–Cretaceous.
Distribution: Worldwide.
Appearance and fossil facts: This is a medium- to large-sized bivalve with an elongate shell. The posterior region of the shell is lengthened and the front area sharply pointed. The ornament is restricted to concentric growth lines. The hinge area is characterized by the presence of a limited number of elongate teeth, and numerous vertical pits for the ligament. *Gervillella* is found in clay-rich sediments. It was a burrower which filter-fed, partially buried in the sediments of the sea-floor. Large specimens of *Gervillella* reach 25 centimetres in length.

Plagiostoma (Lima)

Family: Limidae

Age: Middle Triassic–Late Cretaceous.
Distribution: Worldwide.
Appearance and fossil facts: *Plagiostoma*, previously known as *Lima*, is a medium- to large-sized bivalve. The valves are of equal size, heavy, and have a backward-pointing beak. The hinge line is angular with a small, anterior, wing-like projection. Most specimens are smooth but some species have weak ribs and concentric growth lines. Internally, a single large muscle scar exists in the centre of each valve. Teeth are either weakly developed or absent. A well-defined depression, the lunule, is present on the straight front edge of the shell. Individual shells reach 15 centimetres in size.

Gryphaea

Family: Gryphaeidae

Age: Late Triassic–Cretaceous.
Distribution: Worldwide.
Appearance and fossil facts: The valves of *Gryphaea* are of unequal size, with the left valve larger than the right, and more convex. The beak of the left valve is incurved or rolled over on to the right, lid-like valve, and slightly deflected to

one side. The right valve is flat or slightly concave with a huge muscle scar situated centrally. The larger left valve has a lamellate appearance owing to the deposition of successive layers of shell material. The right valve is often smooth or with a rippled ornament. *Gryphaea* is well known from the Early Cretaceous sediments of the Isle of Wight. Large individuals reach 15 centimetres across.

Ostrea

Family: Ostreidae

Age: Cretaceous–Recent.
Distribution: Worldwide.
Appearance and fossil facts: Commonly known as oysters, the ostreids are among the best-known bivalves throughout the world. They often occur as vast colonies, with myriads of shells accumulated as a shell hash, or lumachelle. The shell of an oyster is often flat, usually orb shaped, and has a layered appearance. The valves can be of different sizes, convex, with an ornament of radial ribs and/or concentric growth lines. A single, large muscle scar occurs in the centre of each valve. Oysters live in shallow, marine and estuarine environments. Individuals reach 15 centimetres in size.

Teredo

Family: Teredinidae

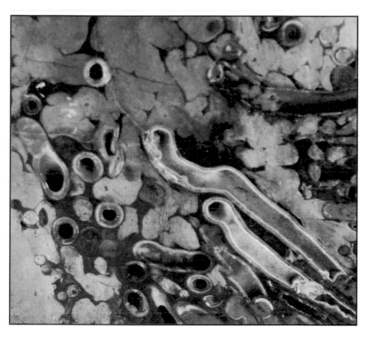

Age: Eocene–Recent.
Distribution: Worldwide.
Appearance and fossil facts: Commonly termed the 'shipworm', *Teredo* is best known from the calcareous linings that it secretes in the burrows it makes in floating timbers. The shell is small, covering the front area of the worm-like body. The valves are T-shaped, with a long hinge. The ornament varies from species to species, but short spines are developed that help the process of boring. The tubes found in fossil wood on the Isle of Sheppey are circular, long, and covered in circular lines. The calcareous material is often white, but a marked sheen is typical of many finds. The tubes can be 15 centimetres in length.

BELEMNITES

Belemnites are cephalopods with an internal skeleton that is divided (from front to back) into a chambered phragmacone, shield-like pro-ostracum and a dense cylindrical guard. The vast majority of belemnite fossil remains are the guards which are composed of resistant calcium carbonate. Belemnites range in time from the Carboniferous into the Tertiary Period.

Hibolites

Family: Hibolitidae

Age: Jurassic–Early Cretaceous.
Distribution: Worldwide.
Appearance and fossil facts: The guard of *Hibolites* expands backwards into an inflated or bulbous posterior region. This gives the specimen its characteristic spearhead or club-shaped outline. A comparatively deep groove is found on the ventral surface. The anterior sections of the skeleton (phragmacone and pro-ostracum) are rarely found but it is common to find numerous specimens of this small belemnite in the Lower Cretaceous clays of southern England. The guard measures 6–8 centimetres in length.

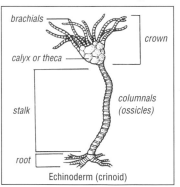

brachials
crown
calyx or theca
columnals (ossicles)
stalk
root
Echinoderm (crinoid)

ECHINODERMS

Commonly known as 'spiny skinned' animals, echinoderms have skeletons made up from calcareous plates. These occur beneath an outer layer of soft tissue. Echinoids may be fixed to the sea-floor or they may be free-living animals. There are five major groups: the sea lilies; sea urchins; starfishes and brittlestars; blastoids. Ancestral echinoderms appeared in Late Precambrian times.

SEA LILIES

Sea lilies (Crinoidea) have cup-shaped thecae with five branched arms that bear hair-like pinnules. Some species are free-living but many have stems and roots. Each component of the skeleton is built of calcareous plates. The first species appeared in the Early Palaeozoic era.

Pentacrinus

Family: Pentacrinitidae

Age: Jurassic.

Distribution: Europe, North America.

Appearance and fossil facts: The stem plates, or ossicles, of *Pentacrinus* are five sided, or pentagonal, in section. They are very distinctive and easily recognizable in Jurassic sediments. *Pentacrinus* is comparatively large although the cup, or theca, is just 1.5 centimetres across. The arms are long with many branches which may extend 15 to 30 centimetres above the cup. The stem is characterized by the presence of regularly spaced, hair-like processes called cirri. In life *Pentacrinus* probably fixed itself to pieces of floating wood, and hung upside-down near the surface of the Jurassic seas.

Marsupites

Family: Marsupitidae

Age: Late Cretaceous.

Distribution: Worldwide.

Appearance and fossil facts: *Marsupites* consists of a large cup, or theca, made up of three rows of polygonal (many sided) plates. The arms are long and narrow, consisting of numerous small plates. Initially the arms are uniserial (single), but they branch symmetrically to form a distinctive crown; there are ten arms. *Marsupites* has no stem or roots; it is thought, therefore, that this animal nestled on the sea-floor, using its arms to gather food. Individual cups grew to 4 centimetres in diameter. Single plates of this crinoid may be used by geologists to help date rocks of the Late Cretaceous Period.

SEA URCHINS

Sea urchins, or echinoids (Echinoidea), are the most commonly found fossil echinoderms. They may be rounded, heart shaped, or slightly elongate animals with a rigid test. The test is divided into ten areas and has a pentamerous (five-fold) symmetry. The mouth of the animal is usually situated on the underside but, in some species, may have migrated across the test and on to the leading edge. The anus is also central in many species but can also migrate laterally in the so-called 'irregular' forms. Spines are typical of many species, and there are

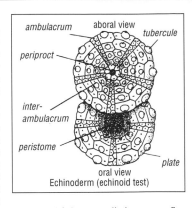

Echinoderm (echinoid test)

then strong bosses that mark their contact areas. Of the ten radiating areas, five bear pores. These are termed ambulacral areas whereas the intervening non-porous areas are called interambulacra. Both areas are made up of two rows of interlocking plates. Spines are characteristic of many echinoids. They articulated with raised bosses found on individual plates.

Hemicidaris

Family: Hemicidaridae

Age: Jurassic–Cretaceous.
Distribution: Europe, North America, Asia, Africa.
Appearance and fossil facts: *Hemicidaris* has a small- to medium-sized, rounded test. The apical area is distinctive, exhibiting five raised plates arranged around a circular opening. Large, strongly developed tubercles exist on the interambulacral plates, with the pored ambulacral areas having a

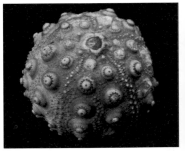

slightly sinuous form. In life, but more rarely in the fossil state, strong spines are attached to the large tubercles. These spines are long, smooth, and taper to a point. Typical tests are 3 centimetres in diameter. A large mouth is present on the underside. *Hemicidaris* lived in shoreline and subtidal environments.

Micraster

Family: Micrasteridae

Age: Cretaceous–Palaeocene.
Distribution: Worldwide.
Appearance and fossil facts:
Commonly known as the Chalk heart urchin, *Micraster* has a distinctive test which has a pronounced anterior notch and a pointed, ridged, posterior region. The pored ambulacral areas are narrow and petaloid, and the test is covered in fine tubercules. The anus is sited below the strong posterior ridge, and the mouth has moved forwards out of the

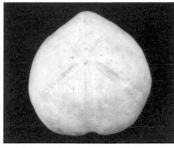

central area. A pronounced lip occurs behind the mouth. *Micraster* is an important zone fossil for the Late Cretaceous. It was a burrowing echinoid. Delicate tube feet drew water into the burrow bringing with it food as well as partly disposing of waste. Excellent specimens of *Micraster* can be found in the Chalk cliffs of England and northern France. A typical test is 5 centimetres in diameter.

Clypeaster

Family: Clypeasteridae

Age: Upper Jurassic–Recent.
Distribution: Worldwide.
Appearance and fossil facts: Adapted to a life partly submerged in sand on the sea-floor, *Clypeaster* has a low-profile test which is flattened on the outer edges. The test is large and strong with five well-developed petal-shaped ambulacra (pored plate areas) on the upper surface. The mouth is central, or almost central, but the anus has migrated to the upper surface. A pentagonal outline is typical of

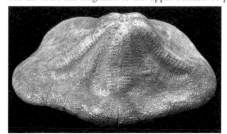

this genus, with the five interambulacral areas being broad and covered with small tubercules. Individual tests measure up to 12 centimetres across. *Clypeaster* is found typically in coarser sediments that were deposited in shallow tropical to subtropical seas.

STARFISHES AND BRITTLESTARS

Starfishes (Asteroidea) and brittlestars (Ophiuroidea) are poorly known from the fossil record. Their skeletons are less robust than those of many other echinoderms, and they tend to disintegrate almost immediately after death. They first appeared during the Ordovician Period.

Starfish

Family: Ophiodermatidae

Age: Palaeozoic–Recent
Distribution: Worldwide.
Appearance and fossil facts: A typical starfish has a relatively small central disc, and five long, robust arms. The disc is made up of ten large plates, and the mouth is sited on the underside. The animal lives on the sea-floor, gathering food with the arms and carrying it into the mouth using hundreds of soft, tube-like extensions. Most complete starfish fossils are associated with fine-grained sediments such as silts and claystones. This suggests that their environment was relatively undisturbed with little or no wave action. Modern-day species also exist in high-energy environments in crevices and reef cavities.

BLASTOIDS

An echinoderm of this group has a bud-like calyx and a well-developed stem. It resembles a fossil rose-bud! The calyx consists of thirteen plates and exhibits a marked radial symmetry. The ambulacra are petaloid and directed downwards from the mouth. Blastoids (Blastoidea) range in time from the Silurian into the Permian Period.

Pentremites

Family: Pentremitidae

Age: Early Carboniferous.
Distribution: North and South America.
Appearance and fossil facts: *Pentremites* is one of the best-known blastoids. The bud-like calyx has a well-developed radial symmetry with the mouth centred on the upper surface. Five spiracles, or outlets, fringe the mouth. The ambulacra are elongate, V shaped, and have well-defined plate grooves lateral to the pores. The calyx is 2 centimetres in diameter. The stem is long with a rooted base. It is composed of plates of ossicles which are locally enlarged to form distinct ring-like features. *Pentremites* lived attached to the sea-floor. Well-preserved specimens are abundant in North America, and many can be found in the fossil shops of Dorset and the north of England.

ARTHROPODS

Having first appeared during the Cambrian Period, the arthropods, or 'jointed-limbed' animals, comprise the largest group of creatures on Earth. The group includes insects, spiders, scorpions, millipedes, centipedes, ostracods, barnacles, and all crustaceans. Several important fossil groups also share the main characteristic: a hard outer skeleton (exoskeleton).

Trilobite (dorsal view)

TRILOBITES

Trilobites are exceptionally well represented during the Palaeozoic Era, with the first species appearing in the earliest part of the Cambrian Period. The external skeleton of a trilobite is divided into a head (cephalon) with a raised middle region known as a glabella, body (thorax), and tail (pygidium); with a characteristic longitudinal division along two well-developed furrows. These extend the length of the body and separate the central axial area from the two lateral lobes. The result is a threefold partitioning from which the group name is derived. The head is usually crescent shaped or semicircular with lateral cheek areas to the sides of the axial region. Facial sutures demarcate free- and fixed-cheek areas. The number of segments in the thorax and tail is diagnostic in identifying different species.

Peronopsis

Family: Peronopsidae

Age: Middle Cambrian.
Distribution: North America, Europe, Asia.
Appearance and fossil facts: Tiny trilobites of the families Agnostidae and Peronopsidae were abundant during the Middle Cambrian Period. The head and tail were of equal size but the thorax consisted of only two or three

thoracic segments. *Peronopsis*, and the agnostids, were blind and there are no eyes present on the head shield area. A distinct rim ran around the edge of the head shield, or cephalon, and the glabella was divided into three distinct lobes. The thoracic segments are clearly defined and may curve backwards slightly. The tail is also rimmed, and the axial area divided into seven or eight lobes. *Peronopsis* and its relatives probably dwelt on the sea-floor in relatively deep waters.

Dalmanites

Family: Dalmanitidae

Age: Silurian–Late Devonian.

Distribution: Europe, North and South America.

Appearance and fossil facts: *Dalmanites* and related genera are important representatives of Palaeozoic marine communities. It is a medium-sized trilobite with the head slightly larger than the tail. The head is semicircular with the glabella marked by deep grooves. It broadens forwards, and is flanked by two well-developed, crescent-shaped, compound eyes. The outer, rear edges of the head shield extend backwards as long genal spines. The thorax consists of eleven segments, each of which is marked by a well-defined pleural furrow. The tail also has eleven segments but these are fused, with the rear margin of the pygidium supporting a long spine. Small tubercules cover the exoskeleton of *Dalmanites*.

Calymene

Family: Calymenidae

Age: Early Silurian–Middle Devonian.

Distribution: Worldwide.

Appearance and fossil facts: The calymenids are medium-sized trilobites. They are often found, like the genus *Phacops*, rolled up for protection, with the tail tucked under the front edge of the cephalon. *Calymene* has a semicircular head with a well-defined glabella and small eyes.

The glabella tapers towards the front of the shield and is strongly lobed. Well-defined facial sutures extend backwards from the front of the head shield around the back of the eyes to cut the genal angle. There are thirteen segments in the thorax, with six distinct rings occurring on the axial region of the fused pygidium or tail. The genus *Flexicalymene* is most commonly found rolled up, and many examples are found every year in Spain and Morocco.

Ogygiocaris

Family: Oxygiocaridae

Age: Early–Middle Ordovician.

Distribution: Europe, North America.

Appearance and fossil facts: Abundant in the slates and claystones of Wales, *Ogygiocaris* is a medium- to large-sized trilobite. The head and tail are of equal size, with the crescentic or semicircular head having short genal spines. The

eyes are comparatively large and crescent shaped, and there is a well-defined facial suture. Eight segments are characteristic of the thorax. The tail is broad with a well-defined axis that tapers to the rear, and fused segments curve backwards. A flattened rim, with semicircular striae, extends around the edge of the pygidium.

Trinucleus

Family: Trinucleidae

Age: Early–Middle Ordovician.
Distribution: Europe.
Appearance and fossil facts: *Trinucleus* has a large head shield and small fused tail. The head is broader than it is long, and the glabella is inflated and expanded towards the front. A fringe of radiating grooves occurs on the leading edge of the cephalon. Long genal spines extend back for twice the length of the body. The thorax consists of six segments. The tail is much wider than it is long, and the segments are relatively poorly defined. Some trinucleids rolled up slightly, tucking the tail forwards under the thorax for protection. These trilobites lived, partially buried in sediments, at the sea-floor.

CRUSTACEA

Fossil crustaceans are poorly known in the fossil record. Crab or lobster beds do occur worldwide but mostly their remains are fragmented by transport or scavenging. Microscopic creatures, such as ostracods, are well preserved, however, in marine and non-marine environments

Centrocythere

Family: Beyrichidae

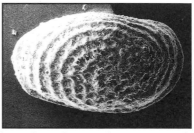

Age: Early Silurian–Middle Devonian.
Distribution: Europe
Appearance and fossil facts: Ostracods are microscopic animals with a two-valved carapace enclosing the soft parts, including jointed limbs. They rarely exceed 5 millimetres across. The valves are articulated along a straight hinge line. The valves are slightly unequal in size and may be smooth or ornamented. *Centrocythere* is strongly ornamented with a nodular or granular surface texture. Ostracods are important in the correlation and dating of rock strata.

Hoploparia

Family: Hoploparidae

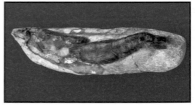

Age: Cretaceous–Eocene.
Distribution: Worldwide.
Appearance and fossil facts: *Hoploparia* is a small lobster with a long, slightly narrow or depressed body. It has long pincers, or chelipeds, and well-defined jointed legs. The skeleton is clearly divided into three regions: the head, thorax, and tail. The head is covered by a long, narrow rostrum. Both thorax and tail are composed of jointed segments. In Britain, lobster beds occur in Cretaceous and in Tertiary strata, with the famous Lobster Beds of the Cretaceous of the Isle of Wight yielding many beautiful specimens. Cementstone nodules on the Isle of Sheppey, off the Kent coast, also contain excellent examples of fossil crustaceans.

Insect in Amber

Insects are very delicate, and their presence in the fossil record is not a true representation of their overall importance since the Late Palaeozoic. Occasionally, exceptional discoveries are made during excavations of very fine-grained sediments deposited in lakes or ponds, or in marine environments inundated by the fine dust produced from volcanoes. Amber, however, the fossilized resin from pine trees and other gymnosperms, is the perfect medium for the entrapment and preservation of insects and spiders. Amber is resistant to weathering, and responds well to polishing. A mosquito in amber had the focal role in recent films featuring the regeneration of the dinosaurs from DNA held in the body of the tiny arthropod.

GRAPTOLITES

The graptolites comprise an extinct group of colonial organisms. They are distant cousins of the vertebrates, and they possess a primitive notochord (flexible rod-like, support structure). The colonies (rhabdosomes) vary considerably, from multiple-branched, fan-shaped structures to a single branch, or stipe. Numerous cup-shaped structures (thecae) occur on each branch. The graptolites evolved during the Early Cambrian Period and survived throughout the Palaeozoic Era.

Dendrograptus

Family: Dendrograptidae

Age: Cambrian–Carboniferous.
Distribution: Worldwide.
Appearance and fossil facts: *Dendrograptus*, and related genera such as *Dictyonema* (*Rhabdinopora*), are most frequently found in Early Palaeozoic slates. These were deposited in deep water, probably outside the continental shelf. The dendroid graptolites were

planktonic, sometimes attached to other organisms. *Dendrograptus* was fern-like in appearance, with the rhabdosome made up of numerous branches. Colonies grew to 6 centimetres across. They are mostly preserved as impressions on bedding planes of rocks. Slates split easily, and excellent examples of dendroid graptolites occur in the Early Palaeozoics of west Wales.

Tetragraptus

Family: Tetragraptidae

Age: Ordovician.

Distribution: Europe, North America, Asia.

Appearance and fossil facts: As the name suggests, *Tetragraptus* has four stipes, or branches. These occur in pairs, and the colony is bilaterally symmetrical. The stipes are lined on the inner edges with numerous tooth-like thecae. These give

each branch a saw-like appearance. *Tetragraptus*, and other graptoloids, evolved rapidly during the Ordovician and Silurian Periods. Successive groups appeared with fewer branches, culminating in the two- and single-branched forms, *Diplograptus* and *Monograptus*. The graptolites are widely distributed, and are important zone fossils for the Early Palaeozoic.*Tetragraptus* colonies measured 2 centimetres across.

Monograptus

Family: Monograptidae

Age: Silurian.
Distribution: Worldwide.
Appearance and fossil facts: *Monograptus* has a single stipe with the thecae arranged along one side. The term used to describe this condition is monoserial. The colonies may be straight, coiled, or spiral, and the thecae tooth-like or long and tube-like in form. Monograptids are particularly abundant in the Baltic region, North America, and in parts of the British Isles. They are very useful zone fossils, and can be used to correlate sediments over huge areas. A typical monograptid is about 3 centimetres long.

VERTEBRATES

Essentially, vertebrates are animals with backbones. Their skeletons are made mostly from bone (calcium phosphate) or cartilage; they are internal although primitive fishes, turtles, and armadillos developed a protective armour to protect the body. The first vertebrates probably evolved in Late Cambrian times.

Cephalaspis

Family: Cephalaspidae

Age: Late Silurian –Devonian.

Distribution: North America –Europe.

Appearance and fossil facts: *Cephalaspis* is an example of an early armoured fish. It had a heavy, bony head shield, and thick scales covered the body. The shield was slightly domed and possessed two backwardly directed horns on the rear corners. A slightly depressed sensory plate area lay inside the front edges of the shield, and there were two eyes on top in the mid-line. *Cephalaspis* was a relatively small, freshwater fish which scoured the bottom sediment in search of food. Cephalaspids are known from the Welsh Borderlands and from Scotland. They grew to 22 centimetres in length.

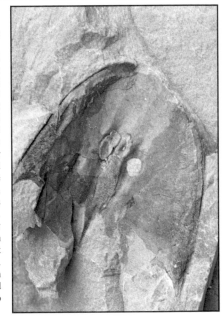

Lamna

Family: Lamnidae

Age: Cretaceous–Pliocene.
Distribution: Worldwide.
Appearance and fossil facts: *Lamna* was a shark, a chondrichthyian, or fish with a cartilaginous skeleton. It is known only from fossilized teeth. A lamnid tooth is small to medium sized, with a large central point and a pair of small side points. The tooth is roughly symmetrical in shape. Sharks have very many teeth, and they tend to

be of different shapes in different areas of the mouth. Some teeth are shed during feeding. A typical lamnid tooth is 2 centimetres long.

Myliobatis

Family: Myliobatidae

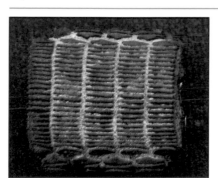

Age: Cretaceous–Recent.
Distribution: Worldwide.
Appearance and fossil facts: *Myliobatis* also has a cartilaginous skeleton. It is a ray which, unlike the sharks, has a battery of robust crushing teeth. The teeth of *Myliobatis* are frequently found in the Tertiary sediments of southern England. They are often lustrous and black in colour. The dental battery or plate is flattened, with each tooth marked by faint striae. The dental plates are divided into files or columns. The widest file is located in the middle. Most people looking for fossils find teeth from the middle file; these are about 3 centimetres across. *Myliobatis* is commonly known as the Eagle Ray, and lives in shallow-water environments.

Lepidotus

Family: Lepidotidae

Age: Triassic–Cretaceous.
Distribution: Worldwide.
Appearance and fossil facts: The robust, isolated scales of *Lepidotus* (*Lepidotes*) are frequently found in sediments of Jurassic to Cretaceous age, particularly in claystones and clay-rich sandstones. This bony fish is rarely found whole, but specimens up to 2 metres in length are known. The scales are shiny, with enamelled surfaces. Sometimes they are found together in longitudinal rows which exhibit a slight overlapping, or imbrication. Individual scales measure 1.5 centimetres.

Turtle

Reptilia

Age: Triassic–Recent.
Distribution: Worldwide.
Appearance and fossil facts:
Turtles, terrapins, and tortoises exist today in marine, freshwater, and land environments. The first representatives of the group appeared in the Triassic Period, and fragments of turtle shell, limb bones, skulls, and even whole shells are, compared with remains of other vertebrates, quite common. In part, this is due to the presence of the

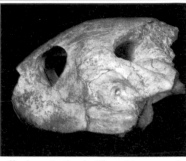

robust shell that encases the body. It affords protection in life and increases the chances of fossilization. The more frequent remains include the patterned scutes of *Trianyx*, a freshwater turtle, and the smoother, more complex plates of marine turtles such as *Eosphurgis* and *Argillochelys*. Plates, skulls, and shells are often found in the Cretaceous to Tertiary sediments of the London and Hampshire Basins.

Crocodile

Reptilia

Age: Triassic–Recent.
Distribution: Worldwide.
Appearance and fossil facts:
Crocodile teeth, scutes, and vertebrae occur in marine and in freshwater sediments. Among the best-known European fossils are *Metriorhynchus* from the Jurassic and *Gioniopholis* from the Jurassic and Cretaceous. Crocodiles are known mainly from isolated bones, and the highly ornamented scutes

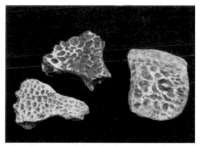

that covered the back are frequently discovered in the Jurassic clays of Bedfordshire and the Tertiary sediments of southern England. Crocodile teeth have short, enamelled crowns and long roots. The vertebrae have robust neural spines, and many have a flat-faced articulation surface (either side of the centrum).

Ichthyosaur

Reptilia

Age: Triassic–Cretaceous.
Distribution: Worldwide.
Appearance and fossil facts: The spectacular skeletons of fish-like ichthyosaurs occupy pride of place in many museums. Their relative abundance depends largely on the existence of several outstanding, or special, faunas scattered throughout the world. In Europe, the collections from the Jurassic of southern Germany and Lyme Regis in Dorset,

England provide us with a unique opportunity to study their morphology and habitat. Complete skeletons continue to be found in the Liassic and Oxford Clay deposits of England and Wales. But isolated teeth, fragments of jaws, and large, flattened, disc-shaped vertebrae are the usual indicators of these beautiful creatures.

Dinosaur

Reptilia

Age: Triassic–Cretaceous.
Distribution: Worldwide.
Appearance and fossil facts: The first dinosaurs were discovered in southern England. The remains of *Megalosaurus*, *Iguanodon*, and *Hyaleosaurus* encouraged Richard Owen to establish the name Dinosauria and, through a name, generate an

ongoing fascination for the past from the general public. Dinosaur bones are found in the Jurassic to Cretaceous sediments of southern England, and spectacular finds have been made recently on the Isle of Wight. Complete specimens are extremely rare but the leaf-like teeth of a sauropod or the serrated teeth of *Megalosaurus* turn up from time to time. Tail vertebrae and large fragments of long bones may also occur locally.

Mammal

Mammalia

Age: Triassic–Recent.
Distribution: Worldwide.
Appearance and fossil facts: Many mammalian fossils are known from their teeth. These are resistant to transport and scavenging, and are relatively common in cave deposits and river gravels. The remains of small, rodent-like creatures occur in the Triassic fissure deposits of the Mendip Hills and in South Wales. But the most common finds are the teeth of horses, deer, and elephants in the gravels of the Thames and other river valleys that have existed over the last 10,000 years or more. Cave deposits in South Wales have yielded the remains of large carnivorous mammals. Caves and river gravels also contain evidence of humans, in the forms of stone tools and, rarely, bones.

TRACE FOSSILS
Trace fossils are the tracks, trails, and burrowing systems formed by animals during feeding processes or in their search for resting or dwelling places. They first appeared in the Late Precambrian (about 600 million years ago).

Skolithus (Dwelling trace)

Age: Cambrian–Recent.
Distribution: Worldwide.
Appearance and fossil facts: *Skolithus* is one of the oldest fossil traces, and is best known as the Pipe Rock of Scotland. The trace consists of vertical, single tubes found in clay-rich sands and sandstones. Single tubes reach a depth of 30 centimetres and range from 2 to 4 centimetres in diameter. They are often closely spaced, and are thought to be the burrows of soft-bodied worms. The burrows are indicative of shallow-water environments where they represent semi-permanent homes for the organisms.

Monocraterion (Dwelling trace)

Age: Mesozoic–Recent.
Distribution: Worldwide.
Appearance and fossil facts: Like *Skolithus*, *Monocraterion* is a single, tube-like burrow that enters the substrate vertically. The burrow is often 3 to 6 centimetres across and up to 30 centimetres in depth. Unlike *Skolithus*, however, this trace is characterized by a ringed structure, each ring reflecting a phase of movement within the burrow. Movements may be

associated with the rate of deposition – the amount of material settling on the sea floor. To avoid being smothered, the animal may have moved upwards leaving a marked trace on the edge of the burrow, These traces are often termed *spreite* or *spreiten*. *Monocraterion* burrows are quite common in the sandy sediments of the Jurassic of Dorset and north-eastern England.

Ophiomorpha (Dwelling trace)

Age: Mesozoic–Recent.
Distribution: Worldwide.
Appearance and fossil facts: *Ophiomorpha* may occur as single or as branched burrow systems. The single burrows are usually vertical, with a 3 to 6 centimetre diameter. They may extend to depths of more than 1 metre into the sediment, but

the deeper burrows are mostly branched with enlarged nodes at turning points. Characteristically, *Ophiomorpha* has a knobbly surface texture, with lumps of sediment stuck by the animal to the internal surface of the burrow. *Ophiomorpha* burrows are usually associated with crabs, lobsters, and shrimps. They are often found in sand-rich sediments. Rarely, they contain the fossilized remains of the animals that helped create them.

Thalassinoides (Dwelling and feeding trace)

Age: Jurassic–Recent.

Distribution: Worldwide.

Appearance and fossil facts: *Thalassinoides* burrows are formed parallel, or just subparallel, to the surface of the sea-floor. In rocks, this surface is known as a bedding plane, and trace fossils, such as *Thalassinoides*, reflect the activity of organisms on or within the sediment on the sea-floor. The burrows of *Thalassinoides* are repeatedly branched, and are cylindrical with slight swellings, or nodes, at the junctions between tubes. Single tubes are 2 to 5 centimetres in diameter and can be 30 centimetres long. The burrows are associated with *Callianassa*, the ghost shrimp. Many burrows may be partially or wholly filled with the droppings of these creatures.

Coprolites (Fossil dung or droppings)

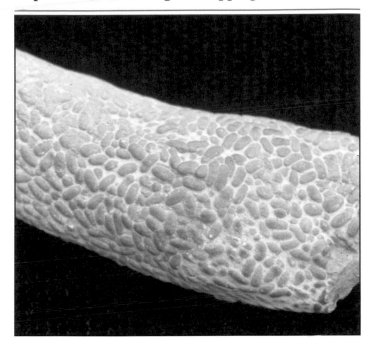

Age: Cambrian–Recent.
Distribution: Worldwide.
Appearance and fossil facts: Coprolites are essentially trace fossils. They are the droppings from all types of animals, and vary in size from a few millimetres to 20 or 30 centimetres long. Droppings associated with gastropods and shrimps can fill burrow systems whereas the distinctive coiled coprolites of fishes or some reptiles are very common in marine deposits. Many coprolites are phosphatic. They often contain evidence of the animals' diets, and are useful in the analysis of ancient food chains. The study of dinosaur coprolites has resulted in the accumulation of a vast and varied collection of material yet to be linked with specific animals.

accessory mineral minor mineral, or mineral phase, present in rock.

amygdale 'almond-shaped', spherical, or ellipsoidal cavity found in lavas.

arenaceous term applied to sandy rocks with a grain size less than 2 mm.

argillaceous term applied to clay- to silt-grade rocks which are very fine grained (<0.0625 mm).

asbestiform specifically used as a descriptive term for the fibrous nature of actinolite. But more generally applied to crocodilite and serpentine.

Baveno well-known example of simple twinning commonly associated with orthoclase feldspar. Right- and left-handed twins can occur in triclinic and monoclinic feldspars.

bipyramidal describes the presence of a pyramidal termination at both ends of a crystal.

Carlsbad well-known type of twin associated with orthoclase feldspar in which the vertical axis is the axis of twinning. Also known as a **penetration twin**.

cement describes a material, such as calcite, which binds together grains in sedimentary rocks. The cement is deposited from mineral-rich waters that percolate through the rock.

clast fragment of broken rock or shell material found in sedimentary rock.

continental platform/shelf a gently sloping surface that passes from the shoreline to the start of the more steeply dipping **continental slope**.

country rock pre-existing rock into which igneous materials are intruded.

cryptocrystalline term desribing rocks or nodules in which the crystal form is too fine to be defined under the microscope.

ductile quality of stretching found in minerals such as gold and silver.

dyke cross-cutting, tabular igneous intrusion which is often vertical or subvertical in relation to surrounding rock.

equigranular term used to describe a rock of equal grain size.

exotic describing materials brought into an area from elsewhere; they include boulders in conglomerates and volcanic bombs in sediments.

fissile describes rocks such as flagstones, slates, and schists which split easily.

flux mineral used to enhance process of smelting slags in metal industry.

fumarole volcanic vent which emits steam, gas, and volatiles at high temperatures.

gangue mineral non-commercial mineral associated with mining. Common gangue minerals are quartz and fluorite.

genal angle angle between the side and back margins of a trilobite headshield.

hydrothermal vein vein filled with minerals precipitated from hot hydrothermal fluids.

immature term used to define the level of transport undergone by a sandstone or other clastic rocks. Immaturity is reflected in the angularity of the constituent grains.

inner platform nearshore area of the surface that dips downwards to the continental slope. Characterized by good light penetration and shallow water depths.

intrusion body of igneous rock that has been emplaced into pre-existing rocks.

lopolith saucer-shaped igneous INTRUSION of variable size.

malleable term used to describe a mineral that tends to flatten or flow rather than fracture if struck hard.

mammilate describing rounded or curved surfaces found in minerals and fossils.

Mannebach type of simple twin found in feldspars.

massive descriptive term used to describe large accumulations of a specific mineral.

metastable mineral (state) which is capable of change to a more stable phase.

mid-platform area in middle of surface

that extends from the shoreline to the CONTINENTAL SLOPE. Characterized by fair to good light penetration and water depths of approximately 60–120 metres.

orogenic belt curved or linear zone which has been subjected to compression, giving rise to mountain chains such as the Andes, Rockies, and Alps.

pelite/pelitic a pelite is a fine-grained, aluminium-rich metamorphic rock derived from shales and mudstones. Pelitic essentially defines the fine-grained, micaceous nature of such rocks.

pelloidal term given to sedimentary rocks in which faecal pellets are abundant.

petaloid term used to describe the petal-like shape of the pore-bearing interambulacra in sea urchins.

plagioclase very important rock-forming silicate.

pleural furrow a furrow that occurs on the outer part of a body segment (pleuron) in trilobites.

plutonic term usually used to describe igneous rocks that have crystallized at great depth.

polypoid term used to describe presence of many sac-like organisms in a colony.

porphyroblast large well-formed crystal that developed in place in a metamorphic rock.

porphyry medium- to coarse-grained igneous intrusive rock with a high percentage of well-formed crystals.

process term used to describe connecting structures between skeletal tissue in tabulate corals.

pseudomorph literally a 'false structure' where a secondary mineral or aggregate of minerals replaces an original mineral without changing the original crystal shape.

rhombododecahedron crystal with a cubic symmetry; having 12 rhomb-shaped faces.

rudaceous describing a sedimentary rock with grains over 2 mm in size.

rudist unique form of extinct bivalve from the Cretaceous, in which the lower, left valve is often very large, and the right valve is lid-like.

sabkha restricted coastal area bordering an enclosed lagoon or saline lake in which evaporation results in the precipitation of minerals such as halite, anhydrite, and borax.

salt-dome circular, rather elongate structure formed by the upward movement of evaporitic minerals such as halite. Extends downwards for several kilometres with the upper part bulb-like and 1–2 km across.

shield area a shield, or craton, is an area of the continental crust that is no longer affected by fold movements. They are ancient areas which have been stable for over 1 billion years; e.g. the Canadian Shield.

sill horizontal or tabular igneous intrusion with regular contacts with the adjacent COUNTRY ROCK.

specific gravity the ratio of the mass of a mineral to the mass of an equal volume of water, expressed as a number.

spherule small spherical particle of volcanic glass or aspherical piece of nickel-iron derived from a disintegrating meteorite.

stock steep igneous intrusion with vertical to sub-vertical sides.

sulcus groove or furrow.

texture defines the shape and size of particles and their interrelationships in a given rock.

turbidite sediment produced as a result of a sudden flow of material downslope from the edge of the CONTINENTAL SHELF.

valve one half of the shell found in bivalves, brachiopods, or ostracods.

vesicular term used to describe rocks, such as basalts, which contain numerous bubble-shaped gas cavities.

vug cavity in rock which is often lined with minerals.

Index